WISER

How To Build And Manage
Wealth God's Way

STEPHEN MARTIN

This book is the result of hundreds of conversations with trusted friends, mentors and coaches and extensive personal study of what the Bible says in regard to how we build wealth while honoring God with our lives. Thank you to each person who helped me discover the biblical truths presented in this book.

To my wife, Kyla: *You've always stood by me as we've built a life together on the principles described in this book. Your unmerited grace and patience have been invaluable in our journey together.*

To my children, Adilyn, Breelyn, and Greyson and to my future children, grandchildren, and great-grandchildren: *I want you to live a life of significance and impact. The principles outlined in this book have served me well and will change your life if you apply them. The best experience is someone else's. My prayer is that you will build your life God's way as you stand on your mother's and my shoulders.*

To Vintage Church: *It is one of my greatest honors to lead and equip you for every good work. My prayer is that you would embrace God's Word and His principles by applying them and, as a result, fulfill your greatest calling in this life.*

TABLE OF CONTENTS

HOW TO USE THIS BOOK IN A GROUP SETTING

Take your study to the next level by discussing what you've learned with a group of friends or a small group. You and your friends or group can dig deeper into the **WISER** life God has for you and learn how to walk in His design.

To really apply this content to your life, you need to bring other people along with you. Discipleship and accountability are the keys to making any spiritual discipline become a living part of your faith walk. As you study the truths contained in **WISER: How To Build And Manage Wealth God's Way,** you'll be able to grow and reach your full potential by surrounding yourself with those whom you can mentor and those who can mentor you.

In the pages that follow each chapter, you'll find devotionals for personal study with Scripture passages, key thoughts, a series of questions for personal reflection, and a journaling section to make this material come alive for you. You may also use these materials to help guide you and your friends in a group discussion about each chapter's topic, using the questions for reflection as a springboard for discussion.

As you study these deeper concepts personally and with trusted friends, you'll be able to take away the principles that will help you grow spiritually and follow God's wisdom for your lives.

Access bonus materials, including teaching videos and other resources at *onechurchresource.com* today!

INTRODUCTION

God wants you to be financially independent, free from the shackles of debt and fear. Whether you're digging yourself out of a financial ditch or planning for the future, now is the time to build on a foundation that endures. True wealth isn't just a matter of what you have. It's about what you do with what you have. My intent in writing this book is to give you biblical principles that you can apply, regardless of your age, context, or economic situation. If you work these principles, they will work for you.

Through the years, I've come to several crossroads in life. I have experienced times where the decisions I've made have impacted my life and my future in big ways.

One of those times was when I first gave my life to Christ. I came to a crossroad when I took a look at the people I was spending most of my time with and realized that if I wanted to continue to grow in my faith and honor God, I had to put myself in a position to be around some people who would help me do that.

Now don't misunderstand me. I do have some friends who are far from God. I think it's good to have people in your life who don't know Christ, but those people shouldn't influence the way you believe or the way you worship. You should be influencing them for God's kingdom. They shouldn't be influencing you to live like the world. When I first accepted Christ, I realized that many of my old friends were holding me back from growing in my relationship with God, so I had to make a decision. Once I changed my friends, I started growing in my faith.

Fast forward ten years later: I was newly married, in a new city, and I got a job that seemed absolutely amazing on the surface. I started making big money. I was selling extended car warranties. I was on the ground-floor of a company, and I was making more money than both my parents and my in-laws combined. If you know me at all, you know I can be pretty persuasive, and I was at the top of the sales charts.

There was only one problem. After a few months, I realized that in order to stay at the top of the sales charts, my colleagues were being strongly encouraged to start bending the truth a bit. Then the pressure started to come my way. I was going to have to stop being so honest about that "full" coverage, if you know what I mean. There I was at another crossroad. Was I going to sacrifice my integrity for a job and money? I had to make a decision. I'm glad to report that I made the right decision to give my two-weeks' notice and to spend my time doing something that honored God and maintained my personal integrity.

You and I are a lot alike. I'll bet that if I sat down to talk to you, you'd tell me about times in your life where you had to make one, two, or maybe three or four decisions that completely altered the course of your life. Maybe you had to break up with your college sweetheart, but later you found the man of your dreams. Maybe you had to pass up that promotion because it would take you away from your family too many days out of the year at a critical time in their lives. Maybe you had to change jobs, change cities, or even change your friends. Because you're a human being, living on planet Earth, I know you have faced a few crossroads in your life. How did you navigate them?

DECIDING WHICH ROAD TO TAKE

Every time I come to a crossroad, whether I have made the right decision or the wrong one, in the end, I always find the same two things to be true.

The first thing I've learned is that it's better to choose to obey God's Word. Even when I didn't feel like it, even when I didn't understand why, I've learned from experience (both good and bad) that it's always better to do things God's way.

As a pastor, I talk to people all the time who say, "I don't really know which way to go."

When I start digging deeper and ask them, "Hey, are you getting to know God? Are you in His Word? Do you believe what He says?" they put their heads down. They go on to admit that knowing God and learning His ways haven't been a priority for them. This is what has led to their confusion, and, admittedly, much of mine over the years. But as you get to know God, He helps you know what to do and which way to go.

If you want to please God and follow Him in these times of decision, you have to learn to say "yes" to the Bible because God's plan is always bigger and better than you can ever imagine. He sees far beyond your decision and ahead into your future, and He knows the way you should go. God isn't just one step ahead of you, but a thousand. He alone knows what will fulfill you today and in the future.

The second thing I've learned is that the longer I follow Jesus, the easier it is to make the right decision at these crossroads. When I obeyed God's Word and did what I knew was right, the Holy Spirit always comforted me and encouraged me. I learned to trust that sense of peace that God's Spirit gave me, and as I got further out, I could look back at that fork in the road and see how much better my life had become because I made the right choice. All the things we are afraid of, all the things we are worried will happen—we won't have those struggles after awhile because God blesses us when we take Him at His Word.

A FINANCIAL CROSSROAD

Sooner or later, the longer you walk with God, you're going to come to a crossroad with your money. Every single believer comes to a place of decision with how they're going to deal with money. I'm not just referring to giving or whether or not you're going to pay your tithes. I'm referring to how you're going to relate to your resources. Are you going to be an out-of-control spender or impulse buyer who is always overly excited in the moment only to get home and become super disappointed? Are you going to be a person who buries yourself in debt? Are you going to be a person who holds everything back because you're afraid you won't have enough? Are you going to be generous? Are you going to be grateful for what you do have and not overly focused on what you don't?

It's inevitable that we'll all come to a crossroad when it comes to resources. Jesus taught that the financial system of this world is at odds with the system of managing resources in the kingdom of God. The two systems are warring with each other.

I wrote this book to help you navigate the financial crossroads and discover that, with God's help, you can live the extraordinary life God promises in His Word. My intention is to give you a solid foundation based on four biblical principles, followed by simple, practical applications of those principles that you can start practicing in your life today. I encourage you to view this book as an introduction into each of the principles discussed and to seek out the advice of others, including the abundant resources that are available to help you build wealth God's way.

This book is *NOT* intended to give you every answer to your own unique financial situation. There are volumes of budgeting books, blogs, podcasts, and personal finance materials that will help you develop a system for managing your money. I'm not trying to give you "ten quick steps to whip your finances into shape," or "three rules for investing your money in the stock market for maximum R.O.I." Much more qualified financial experts can help you with the details of how to set up your budget and stick to it, how to build up your savings account, how to invest your money wisely, and how to maximize your revenues. **That's not the purpose for this book at all.**

My purpose in writing this book is to give you **biblical principles** that will point you in the right direction. The book is a springboard to launch you into taking a more biblical and a more active role in managing the resources God has given you.

It's up to you to take the principles from God's Word, to fully educate yourself, and to put your knowledge to work in your unique circumstances. Join a small group or take a class on how to manage your personal finances, and learn what you need to know to become a good steward of the resources God has entrusted to you. It's never too late to learn something new. That part is completely up to you.

It is my sincere prayer, however, that as you read this book, you will allow God to move in your life by adjusting your perspective to His perspective—that you will become **WISER**.

I believe that as you learn and walk in the biblical principles for becoming a wise steward of God's resources, you will be able to fully experience His best for you in this life.

God bless you on your journey!

Stephen

SECTION 1

THE PRINCIPLES

The first four chapters of this book provide four principles that are foundational pillars to build and to steward wealth God's way. Each one is necessary to create a lasting legacy for your family and for future generations.

SECTION NOTES

CHAPTER 1

WISDOM GUIDES

No one can serve two masters; for either he will hate the one and love the other, or else he will be loyal to the one and despise the other. You cannot serve God and mammon.

Matthew 6:24 NKJV

Jesus said there is a crossroad when it comes to our financial life, where we must choose whether we're going to trust in God or trust in *mammon*. Some of you may be looking at the word *mammon* and wondering what it means. It's an Aramaic word that actually means *riches*. Are you going to trust in God, or are you going to trust in your own resources?

When you study the word *mammon,* at the root, it's closely related to the word "amen." Saying "amen" to something isn't just religious tradition. When you say "amen" to something, you're actually saying, "Yes, I agree. That can be trusted." You're agreeing and acknowledging your belief in whatever was said. The concept of mammon that Jesus discussed in the context of Matthew 6:24, is not whether we can have riches (or resources), it's whether we're going to trust in them. Where is our trust going to rest? Is it going to be with God as our ultimate Provider? Or is our trust going to be placed in our *stuff?*

Put simply, does your peace of mind come from your bank account and all of your possessions, or does it come from God?

You may be thinking, *Well, Pastor, If I had more money, I'd have more peace of mind.*

But would you really?

The trust in mammon goes both ways. Whether your bank account is high or low, trusting in your possessions is a double-edged sword. If your bank balance is high, you may think, "Man, I'm good to go. Everything's taken care of. Life is good." But then when it's low or the economy is down, you may get worried about how you're going to keep what you have. Jesus was saying we can't let our stuff, or lack thereof, determine our peace of mind.

It isn't that God doesn't want us to have good things. It's that He doesn't want our things to have the power to determine our peace. **It's a matter of trust, not a matter of stuff.** God is opposed to us trusting in our stuff instead of trusting in Him.

Jesus illustrates this in a story found in Mark's Gospel.

In this particular passage, Jesus was sitting down in front of the collection box watching as people dropped their money into the chest. (Aren't you glad we don't do that today? We just pass a bucket in a dimly-lit room during church.) Here, Jesus wasn't just watching. He was also discerning the motives of the people who were giving.

> Jesus sat down opposite the place where the offerings were put and watched the crowd putting their money into the temple treasury. Many rich people threw in large amounts. But a poor widow came and put in two very small copper coins, worth only a few cents. Calling his disciples to him, Jesus said, "Truly I tell you, this poor widow has put more into the treasury than all the others. They all gave out of their wealth; but she, out of her poverty, put in everything—all she had to live on."

> Mark 12:41–44 NIV

Let's just stop and think about that for a moment. Where was the widow's trust? Was her trust in those two coins that she was giving to the Temple? Where was her trust? It obviously wasn't in her money because Jesus said, "She gave out of her need."

One of the ways you can overcome your attachment to worldly riches is to be generous toward God and His kingdom. Generosity cuts the string that's attached between your heart and your stuff. The widow understood that there was a powerful principle to be found in giving out of your need.

During His ministry on Earth, Jesus talked about money and possessions more than any other topic. Money and possessions are talked about in the Bible more than faith, love, hope, joy, and peace are talked about all combined. Why? Because there's something inside of our flesh that causes our hearts to attach themselves to our stuff. In Matthew 6:24, Jesus was telling us, "That's really going to mess up your relationship with Me because you can't serve two things at the same time. Your heart can't be attached to possessions and to Me. It won't work." That's why Jesus talks about money a lot. Following in His footsteps, I think God's people should have a lot of honest conversations about money too.

As a pastor, I usually teach this topic from the side of generosity and giving. I don't think there's anything wrong with that. I think God's people should be generous with others and with the house of God. Teaching about giving is good, but that's only one side of the coin when it comes to the topic of money (no pun intended). It's really not even the first thing we should know when we start thinking about what or whom we're going to trust. No, we need to have even deeper conversations about how we're going to interact with our finances. We need to broaden our perspective.

GOD'S WAY OR THE WORLD'S WAY?

For us to get the whole picture of how God wants us to handle resources, we have to back up and look at systems. (Don't worry, I'm not going to get all nerdy and make your eyes glaze over with a bunch of charts and spreadsheets!) We just need to get a good overview of how God wants us to interact with stuff.

I said earlier that God has a system, and the world has a system. The mammon system is based on putting your trust in riches and possessions. But the system of handling resources God's way is different. God's system is in direct opposition to the world's system of obtaining and sustaining wealth. As a matter of fact, it's so different, that a lot of people—even good, Christian people who go to church, read their Bibles, and pray every day—don't understand how it works.

I don't think the problem in the Church is that God's people are stingy or greedy. At least that's not the case for the believers that I've met. Sure, a couple of them are stingy, but for the most part, the Christians I know are some of the most generous people I've ever met. Most of them give whatever small amounts they can give to help make room for more people to come into the kingdom of God. They really want to do more, but they just can't.

I refuse to believe that Christians as a whole are greedy or stingy. That's not the issue. I think the real issue is that they want to do more, but most of the people in the Body of Christ are just broke. We're strapped. We struggle to understand how God's financial system works. But I have good news for you. It doesn't have to be that way.

GIVING AND RECEIVING

I don't think you would argue if I told you that it's God's will that we not only give but that we also receive. In the church, preachers talk a lot about giving, but if we're going to be positioned by God to give the way God has called us to give, we have to learn to receive from Him first. No matter how much we may want to give, it's impossible to give if we don't understand how to receive.

So how do receive from God?

Receive my instruction [wisdom], and not silver, And knowledge rather than choice gold.

Proverbs 8:10 NKJV, Author's note

Another translation says, "Love my wisdom and hate silver and gold."

That seems kind of harsh. *Hate* silver and gold? Is God telling us to go back to the barter system and trade cows, pigs, and our stuff so we can do away with money?

No, thankfully, that's not what He's saying.

Proverbs 8:10 is written as an idiom. It's a famous saying in the Hebrew language.

We have sayings that are similar in English. Growing up, when my mom would get upset about something, I'd say, "Mom, don't have a cow!" Was my mother ever in danger of actually calving? Of course not. It was just my way of telling her I thought she was overreacting. (Although looking back now, I'll admit she probably was reacting appropriately to whatever challenging situation I had put her in at the time.) "Don't have a cow," is just an idiom.

Proverbs 8:10 is an idiom too. When Solomon tells us we should love wisdom and hate silver and gold, he's saying that God's wisdom is better than any stuff (silver and gold included) that you could ever have. God is telling us that, by comparison, wisdom is so much better. You and I should live and breathe to reach and obtain wisdom because, in God's wisdom—understanding His system and plan—everything we need will be taken care of.

HOW GOD PAYS US BACK

If there was ever a book for you to read from cover to cover, this is it. In the pages that follow, you're going to learn the key principles behind a different system than the world's system for handling your finances—a system that's going to make you **WISER.**

Did you know that every economy has a currency? If an economy didn't have a currency, there would be absolute chaos. Imagine if we woke up this morning and there was no money in our bank accounts, and our debit cards didn't work. Can I just tell you, we would run out of gas and groceries pretty quickly? There would be a run on the banks, gas stations, grocery stores, water, and more. It would be a mess!

Even if we didn't use the dollar for currency here in the United States, there would still be some form of currency that had value assigned to it. In the ancient world, people operated on a barter system. (For those of you who love Facebook Marketplace, they're trying to bring that system back.) If you had a chicken but you really wanted a cow, you would have to wait for somebody who had a cow to really want a chicken. You might have to wait until you had two or three chickens to get a small cow, but when someone else really wanted chickens, you could trade.

How incredibly ineffective and inefficient that would have been. As people groups grew and their economies evolved, that's why they started dealing with coins. Coins brought a set value based on a single standard into societies. And that led to paper-based currencies. Our own currency used to be based on what was called, the "Gold Standard," meaning that for every paper dollar that was in circulation, there was an equal amount of gold stored in a place like Fort Knox or one of the other repositories around the country to back it. (Things work differently now, but that's not the topic of this book, so we'll just move along.) The point is that the purpose of currency in any society is to bring that economy a standard.

Just as the economy of America is based upon the currency of the dollar, when we study the economy of God, we need to recognize that it also has a currency. This is where it becomes difficult for us to understand. Because we live in this worldly economy, always trading dollars for stuff, it's hard for us to wrap our minds around the fact that His currency is not the same as our currency. It's not paper, coins, or stuff. That brings us to the question: What is the currency of the kingdom of God? The currency of God's economy is wisdom.

Wisdom is how we receive things from God.

Wisdom is the tool God uses to get resources to us.

THE CURRENCY OF WISDOM

The exchange of wisdom is the currency of the economy of God. So, let's look at a few principles concerning wisdom.

1.   **Wisdom comes before blessing.**

Wisdom comes first because it was first. Wisdom was established before the material world was ever created.

> The Lord formed me [wisdom] from the beginning, before he created anything else. I was appointed in ages past, at the very first, before the earth began.
>
> Proverbs 8:22–23 NLT, Author's note

The world lives under a false belief that science and God are at odds, but nothing could be further from the truth. I married a physician, and she's brilliant. My wife loves science, and every time she learns more about science, it draws her closer to God. The God of the supernatural is also the God of the natural.

Where do you think all the laws of physics that hold our entire world together came from? The Bible says they were established in the beginning. If the wisdom of the laws of physics weren't established, nothing would be held together. There would be no gravity. Everything would exist in a state of chaos. Even if humanity existed, we wouldn't be able to function. God is Omniscient. He possesses all wisdom, all knowledge of scientific principles. The laws of physics are the supreme manifestation of God's wisdom.

Science and God don't contradict each other. They complement each other. Science points to how big our God is and to how much wisdom He possesses, and the Bible says that the wisdom of God came first.

Wisdom always comes first. Wisdom came before the world was formed. Wisdom comes before blessing. Wisdom comes before money. Wisdom always precedes the manifestation of what we're looking for. It's a spiritual law. If God's people don't understand this principle, we'll be looking for money to meet our needs, and we'll miss wisdom. Instead of waiting for Publisher's Clearing House to show up with a big pay out or waiting for our numbers to be called in the lottery, we need to recognize that wisdom is the currency of God's economy.

I meet a lot of Christians who believe that because they just gave to the building fund or started tithing that God is going to direct people they don't even know to start handing them money or mailing them big checks. And then they get disappointed and quit giving because they missed this very important principle: **God doesn't pay us back with dollars because that's not the currency of His economy.**

So while we're looking for the check, there's someone outside the front door with the answer to everything we need. His name is Wisdom, and he's knocking on the door, but because we don't recognize that he's God's answer, we miss the many opportunities he provides for future blessing. Wisdom always precedes blessing.

2. **Wisdom is better than money.**

We think we need more stuff, but *more* isn't always the answer. God, in His omniscience, knows what we really need because He sees every problem we have—even the ones we don't know about yet. Wisdom sees so much further out. Wisdom doesn't just meet your present needs, but it also meets your future needs.

> I [wisdom] have riches and honor, as well as enduring wealth and justice.
>
> Proverbs 8:18 NLT

With wisdom, wealth lasts and is honest. Without wisdom, wealth is fleeting and deceitful. Have you ever been taken advantage of financially? For example, maybe some slick-talking salesman on the phone over-sold you an extended car warranty. Your car wasn't even worth what the warranty cost, but they assured you that you would have full coverage over any part that broke down. But then you went to the dealership to get something fixed. You thought the coverage was "bumper-to-bumper," but you found out it was only "comprehensive," which pretty much meant the warranty didn't cover anything. Would that make you feel good? Would it make you feel powerful? No! You'd want to get even with that jerk on the phone! (That's why I don't sell extended car warranties anymore!)

When we apply God's wisdom to our situations, it's better than any guarantee of future blessing or any short-term gain of money. Because it's honest. Wisdom can be trusted. Instead of looking for the latest life hack or get-rich-quick scheme, we can live a blessed life because of an honest exchange of goods in the economy of this world when we apply God's wisdom to our lives.

Sometimes people come to me and say things like, "Pastor, I paid my tithe, but I haven't seen any money back from God. Tithing doesn't work!" But again, they don't understand the principle of wisdom in God's economy. God doesn't pay us back with paper bills or metal coins that will one day tear, disintegrate, or rust. He pays us back with a commodity that cannot be diminished over eons of time. **God pays us back with wisdom in the form of ideas.** It's up to you when He gives you the ideas to flesh them out. It's up to you to make them happen.

Ideas turn into money. Money comes from creative ideas— but not just from *having them*. The blessing comes from *acting on them*.

First you get the wisdom in the form of creative ideas, and then you have to put those ideas to work.

> And God is able to bless you abundantly, so that in all things at all times, having all that you need, you will abound in every good work.
>
> 2 Corinthians 9:8 NIV

As you listen to it and put it to work, God's wisdom will guide you in those situations that haven't even happened yet. Hard work is an important part of your solution, but it's incomplete by itself. Hard work has to be joined with *smart* work.

If you're like everyone else, there are some things about your job that are mundane. You do them over and over, and over again. But then you have a thought, "Hey, there might be an easier way to do this." Then you try that idea, and, all of a sudden, you've shaved an hour off your workday. Now you have a free hour to choose to do something else. *That's wisdom.* You may not realize it, but that's God paying you back for being faithful or listening to Him in some area.

Hard work is necessary and important, but God wants us to work *smart* as well. You could be a worker for the county and your job could be to dig sixty-five ditches. You could work for countless days with a shovel and a bucket, but that's not the best way to dig ditches (unless you really love digging ditches by hand). Is there a better way to dig them? Of course, there is. You dig them with a backhoe. That's smarter.

Somebody was out digging a ditch, breaking their back one day, and they saw a car driving by and said, "I wonder if we could harness something similar to dig this ditch faster..." That was wisdom. What if the guy in the ditch had just kept saying, "I can't stop to think right now. I just have to dig this ditch so that someone will give me a check. It's hot out here, but I'm just going to keep doing this for years so I can get my pension. Then I can retire and do what I really want to do."?

Let's not make the same kind of mistake. Let's work hard, but let's always be looking for wisdom. Let's become **WISER.**

3. **Wisdom is the channel of God's blessing.**

Hopefully you're getting the picture here. God doesn't pay us back with money. He pays us with the currency of wisdom. It's God's wisdom that creates channels for His blessings in our lives.

> "Bring all the tithes into the storehouse so that there will be enough food in my Temple. If you do," says the Lord of Heaven's Armies, "I will open up the windows of heaven for you. I will pour out a blessing so great you won't have enough room to take it in! Try it! Put me to the test!"
>
> Malachi 3:10 NLT

That's a powerful passage of Scripture. God says, "You do this. I'll do that." And that's what we usually focus on. Simple instructions. God tells us our part, and He tells us His part. I've taught that verse for years, and that's what I've always seen, but one day, I was talking to someone older, wiser, and wealthier than me, and he showed me another principle in that verse that I had never really noticed before.

We teach this: "When you tithe, God's going to prosper you and give you money in return."

But that's not what it says.

What does God do when we honor Him with the tithe and take Him at His Word? **He opens up windows.** When you open up a window in your house, light and fresh air is channeled into your dark room. A window is a **channel** we can receive things through. As we honor God with our finances, He opens channels of wisdom for us to receive things from Him in return. Wisdom is a channel God uses to get blessings to us. He doesn't drop rolls of bills and buckets of coins on our heads. No, He opens the channels of His wisdom to flow freely to us. Then we have to do our part to turn that God-given wisdom into natural, physical resources. How do we do that? We learn to operate in the fourth principle of wisdom. We have to convert it.

4. **Wisdom has to be converted.**

> Therefore, brethren, be all the more diligent to make certain about His calling and choosing you; for as long as you practice these things, you will never stumble.

> 2 Peter 1:10 NASB

In and of itself, wisdom is a raw material. It won't benefit us if we don't understand what to do with it. We can get all the wisdom from God that we could ever need, but until we act on it and practice it, wisdom's worth remains hidden and unrealized. It's up to us to cultivate channels that connect the wisdom God gives us to our natural world. God will give us wisdom, **AND** He will show us how to apply it in our lives.

Let's look at a natural example to explain this spiritual truth. When it's a hundred degrees outside in the summer where I live in Central Texas, my house has air conditioning. I'm not sure my family would survive without our air conditioning system. Likewise, when it's a cold day in the middle of January, we can flip a switch on the thermostat and make our house nice and warm inside with our central heating system. How does that cool air in the summer and warm air in the winter get into our house from the heating and air conditioning system? It comes through a channel—or to be more precise—through a system of channels, called ductwork, which is connected to electricity that has been converted into usable power to work in our home.

But it doesn't stop there. What happens on the other side of our heating and air conditioning system? Another conversion happens. Electricity and natural gas are distributed to our house through another system of channels, where they are converted into energy. If we look at the electricity that is being converted into energy, there's another conversion. Either coal is being converted into energy, hydroelectric power is harnessing the raw force of a water supply, or a wind turbine is harnessing raw energy and converting it into usable electricity to keep our home cool. Raw energy has to be converted to be useful. There's a lot of electricity in a bolt of lightning, but it isn't converted into usable energy, and it doesn't benefit you if you're in its path. (Wisdom in the wrong hands can be dangerous too.)

In a similar way that the electricity in my house comes through a channel and has to be converted to be usable, the supply of wisdom comes to us from God through channels He opens, but we must convert it to gain the benefit of it in our lives. We'll look specifically at how to convert wisdom in the next chapter, but at this point, we need to understand that when we get wisdom, it's in raw form.

Our perspective can be so limited. Too often we're only looking at what we think we can produce with our own hands. We live hand to mouth and let our bank accounts dictate our actions, but that's not God's plan for us. **God's plan is that we become *WISER*.**

As we continue taking steps to become *WISER* about how we handle our resources, we need to keep these four principles in mind:

» **Wisdom is the tool God uses to get resources to us.**

» **Wisdom comes before blessing.**

» **Wisdom is better than money.**

» **Wisdom is the channel of God's blessing.**

» **Wisdom has to be converted.**

KEY THOUGHTS

» Wisdom is the tool God uses to get resources to us.

» Wisdom comes before blessing.

» Wisdom is better than money.

» Wisdom is the channel of God's blessing.

» Wisdom has to be converted.

CHAPTER 1

WISDOM GUIDES

SMALL GROUP AND DEVOTIONAL LESSONS

◠◠◠◠◠ READ ◠◠◠◠◠

No one can serve two masters. As a Christian, you're eventually going to come to a crossroad in regard to your stuff. Will you trust in the world's economy or God's economy? The world's system is dominated by the fear of not having enough and pits you against others in a battle between those who have resources and those who don't. **God's plan is that we become *WISER*.**

The currency of God's economy is wisdom. It's the tool He uses to pay us back. We don't just need more money, we need more of God's wisdom to build and steward wealth. In God's economy, the sky is the limit, and there's no cap on what God can do in our lives. We can trade scarcity and fear for abundance and peace.

At times we may become shortsighted or hyper focused on our current needs and fail to apply the practical wisdom of God's Word in our lives. **But wisdom always comes before blessing.** It allows us to build on a foundation that lasts for generations. In His infinite wisdom, God designed His blessings to come to us through channels. While we are looking for a check or financial windfall, God gives us wisdom that, when applied, not only meets our needs in the moment, but also sets us up for the future. **Wisdom is a channel for God's blessing.**

- -

☐ **DAY 1**   **Proverbs 1 and 1 Samuel 1**

☐ **DAY 2**   **Proverbs 2 and 1 Samuel 2**

☐ **DAY 3**   **Proverbs 3 and 1 Samuel 3**

☐ **DAY 4**   **Proverbs 4 and 1 Samuel 4**

☐ **DAY 5**   **Proverbs 5 and 1 Samuel 5**

☐ **DAY 6**   **Proverbs 6 and 1 Samuel 6**

☐ **DAY 7**   **Proverbs 7 and 1 Samuel 7**

○○○○○ REFLECT ○○○○○

1. Why is wisdom superior to money in God's economy? In what ways has God opened up channels of blessing in your life?

2. Can you think of a time where you didn't act with God's wisdom, and it affected your finances?

○○○○○ WRITE ○○○○○

Journal your thoughts from the discussion questions here.

_____

_____

_____

_____

_____

_____

_____

_____

_____

_____

_____

_____

_____

_____

_____

_____

CHAPTER NOTES

CHAPTER 2

DILIGENCE BUILDS

Have you ever tried to talk God into doing something for you that you weren't really sure He wanted to do? Have you ever prayed about a need or a situation, but in the back of your mind you really questioned whether or not it was God's will to answer your prayer? I remember when I gave my life to Christ for the very first time. I was new in the faith, and I had this immature attitude about God, particularly in how I prayed and constantly asked Him to bless me.

Parents, you know what this feels like. Your kids come to you with that sweet, innocent smile, wearing your favorite little outfit that you bought them. They look so adorable and cute, and they tell you how much they love you. What are they trying to do? They're trying to get you to take them to Target again! You know they're working you over, but it's hard to resist.

That's how I was with God. "God, if you'll just do what I want you to do for me, then I'll be happy." But as I started reading the Bible, going to church, and getting around people who were more mature in their faith, I discovered that there are certain things written in the Bible you don't have to ask God to bless. He already blesses them. There are things in the Word of God that are guaranteed to bring you blessings.

As we look at our financial situations, what we're able to do or what we're struggling with, we might find ourselves lacking. But God has a better plan for us than that. Instead of telling God our plans and asking for His blessing, we simply need to get with His plan because He's **WISER.**

> "For my thoughts are not your thoughts, neither are your ways my ways," declares the Lord. "As the heavens are higher than the earth, so are my ways higher than your ways and my thoughts than your thoughts."
>
> Isaiah 55:8–9 NIV

God has something so much bigger and better for you than you could ever imagine, but we have to understand this vital truth about how His kingdom operates. **The way to experience God's blessing in your life (financial or otherwise) is to find out what God blesses, and get behind what He's already blessing.**

The Bible is full of things that God blesses and things that He won't. There are things that, no matter how hard you pray, no matter how long you pray, God will never, ever bless.

» **One of the things God won't bless is fear.** When we read stories about the men and women God used to do incredible things, many times an angel of the Lord appeared to them. When that happened, usually the first words out of the angel's mouth were, "Fear not. Do not be afraid." Why is that? Because God cannot use us when we're constantly full of fear. The thing He does use is faith. (See Hebrews 11:6.) God blesses faith, but He will not bless fear. We will dig deeper into the role of faith later, in chapter four.

» **Another thing God won't bless is unforgiveness.** According to Jesus, we shouldn't go through life holding grudges against every person who has done us wrong. God can't bless us if we do. (See Matthew 6:15.) As children of God, we have to learn to get over stuff. That doesn't mean God approves of the wrong things someone may have done. God understands that we've been hurt, but refusing to forgive is as if we're saying God isn't big enough to help us overcome our pain. On the other hand, God blesses forgiveness because it puts our focus on Him and acknowledges that He's bigger than anything another human can do to us.

» **Another thing God won't bless is envy.** This one is usually tied to our finances in some way or another. We may be envious that someone has what we wanted, or someone got the raise we think we deserved or the promotion that should have been ours. God won't bless us when we operate in envy. When we envy another person's blessings or position, it's as if we're telling God, "Lord, you're small. You can only bless one person at a time. I don't believe You can bless me too." At its root, envy is really a lack of faith in God as our Provider. God blesses faith, and envy can never bring us what we want.

While God won't bless fear, unforgiveness, or envy, there are things God always blesses. One of those things is also the primary method for converting God's wisdom into financial blessing. It's diligence.

GOD BLESSES DILIGENCE

The dictionary defines *diligence* as *the quality of persevering.* I like to define it as *work, hustle, move, getting after it, or drive.* It's possessing the character quality of "stick-to-it-iveness." You stick to a task even when it's hard. You won't give up. You're careful in your work and pay attention to details because the details matter. You're industrious.

As I mentioned in the last chapter, it's not enough to work hard; you have to work hard and smart. That's being industrious. The opposite of diligence is laziness.

> Lazy hands make a poor man, but diligent hands bring wealth.

> Proverbs 10:4 TLV

As you've probably heard, there's no such thing as a free lunch. There is no such thing as entitlement. Someone had to be *un*-entitled so that you could be entitled. There's no such thing as get rich quick or windfall wealth that lasts. This can be difficult for us to understand because we live in a world where we can turn on the T.V. or look through our social media feeds and see what other people have. It has never been easier to look inside the life of another person and become envious. Here's the problem with that: We don't get to see the entire process. We won't see any of their struggles. We don't see all their pain. We can't see the years they spent in obscurity before they became an "overnight" success. We can see all the stuff they have, but we can't see what it took for them to get it.

My wife and I are originally from Tulsa, Oklahoma, but we moved away in 2005, and ever since then we've driven back for different holidays, vacations, and hunting trips. As we've driven back several times over the years, I started to notice something interesting. Years ago, when we first started making the drive, I noticed there were little casinos popping up in gas stations all over the place. Those gas stations had slot machines in them and a few neon lights, and they promised a big payday. Some of them were so small, they only had porta-potties outside. They didn't even have indoor plumbing. But every year we would make that drive, I noticed that it seemed as if these little venues were getting an upgrade.

The next few years along the drive, I noticed that these casinos weren't attached to the gas stations anymore; they *were* the gas stations. The gas pumps had become secondary to the casinos, and the signs had gotten bigger. Over the following few years, the little buildings with the gas pumps outside had become bigger buildings—and, boy, they were nice!

I was driving home to go hunting a few months ago, and when I got to the first stop sign in town. I looked to my right and saw what I thought was probably the biggest building in the whole state of Oklahoma in the place of one of the old gas stations. It was a casino, and more! It was an event center with big-name performers. It had strings of lights across acres of parking lots and billboards for miles all around selling the idea that you could have everything you had ever dreamed of having if you just got lucky enough inside. It was wild. I was staring at this building in the middle of rural Oklahoma that should have been at the center of the Las Vegas strip. Wow, how things change!

Then I looked in the parking lot, and I saw the funniest thing. There were hundreds of broken-down vehicles. The hubcaps were missing. They had rust and dents all over them and looked like they had to be towed into place. There was this magnificent edifice surrounded by junkers of every make and model. If you looked at the scene closely, you'd realize the marketers were not delivering on their promise. So why are they still in business? How do they keep getting people to spend their entire paychecks there? People are willingly handing over their hard-earned money because they're selling this promise: *You can have right now what it took thirty years for your parents to get.*

That's an incredibly unbiblical perspective.

"But, Pastor, I like the casino."

If that's what you want to do with your spending money, that's your choice. I don't think it's necessarily ungodly to go to the casino. I just think it's stupid.

I know that hurts, but I'm trying to help you see what God blesses and what He doesn't. Instead of asking God to give you the winning Powerball numbers, get behind what you know God blesses, and you'll be a winner in His kingdom.

WHAT DO YOU WANT TO BE WHEN YOU GROW UP?

My wife, Kyla, and I love to talk to young people. I love asking little kids, "What do you want to be when you grow up?" And they usually say something like, "I want to be a firefighter," or "I want to be an astronaut," or "I want to be a quarterback." They almost always list really difficult professions. I usually pat them on the head and think to myself, Yeah, that's probably not going to happen. Maybe one of them might be able to do something like that, but it's very unlikely.

When the kids get a little older and are in high school, my wife will usually ask the questions, and the conversations go something like this.

"What do you want to be?" Kyla will ask.

A lot of kids know that Kyla's a medical doctor, so they'll tell her, "I want to be a doctor, like you."

"Really?" she'll say. "What kind of doctor?"

"I want to be a neurosurgeon."

"Wow. That's powerful," she'll say. Then she'll follow up with, "So how are your science classes going?"

"Well, I don't really like science."

"Hmmm. Okay," Kyla will continue. "How are your grades?"

"Well, you know, I had kind of a rough spell last year. I'm really going through something, and the teacher doesn't really get me. I'm rocking a 2.0 grade point average."

At this point Kyla's thinking to herself, *Yeah, right. There's not a chance you're going to become a neurosurgeon.*

What those high schoolers don't know about is the thirteen years with residency Kyla had to go through before she could ever become a medical doctor. They don't understand all of the sacrifices she had to make. It's not just about being smart. Kyla had to be diligent for a very long time to become a doctor, and she has to be diligent every day to stay a doctor.

DILIGENCE IS THE KEY

It's not enough to have wisdom. If you don't understand diligence, you can get all the wisdom in the world, but you'll still be broke. You'll still be struggling because **diligence is what converts the wisdom of God into financial blessing.** We have to understand how we can use diligence to bring God's blessings into this natural realm. There are five key principles we have to know to operate in diligence.

1.   **Diligence is a learned behavior.**

Are your children born wanting to wash the dishes? Are they born ready to clean the house from top to bottom? Are they born as natural landscapers? Does attention to detail come naturally for your kids? Of course not.

Lazy people sleep soundly, but idleness leaves them hungry.

Proverbs 19:15 NLT

Do you know why teenagers sleep so well? Because their parents pay for their dinner, that's why! We have to teach our kids to work. Diligence is a learned behavior. And, unfortunately, it's not just an issue for kids. Many adults have never learned the importance of diligence either.

It's natural to be unmotivated. Have you ever met anyone who said, "I just love working out"? If you love working out, you're weird. (Or you're in a cult called CrossFit!) Nobody likes working out.

Choosing to do something takes more than just feeling like doing it. It takes diligence, and diligence is learned. It takes diligence to do things for the bigger, better reason when you don't want to do them.

2. Wisdom and diligence are two sides of the same coin.

You can be diligent but still be unwise. You can work really hard but not use wisdom. As I said before, God wants you to work hard and smart.

When diligence is combined with wisdom, it makes you unstoppable.

But he who looks into the perfect law of liberty and continues in it, and is not a forgetful hearer but a doer of the work, this one will be blessed in what he does.

James 1:25 NKJV

It's not just hearing (or learning) something. You have *to do* what you learned to be blessed.

On a side note, many people believe that God wants to hold things back from them and to take away their fun. Nothing could be further from the truth. James tells us that the Bible is "the perfect law of liberty." When we apply God's laws to our lives, we become free. If you're a slave to a sin, a slave to the opinions of others, or a slave to living paycheck to paycheck, God wants to set you free. That's why He gave us His Word. It's so powerful. We have to change the way we think about the Bible.

James says that knowing and continually doing God's Word is a recipe for success that the casinos cannot deliver. Only wisdom with diligence brings God's blessings.

3. **Diligence is about your character, not about your personality.**

It's easy to quit when things get tough, but it takes tremendous character to stay. It's easy to change jobs when the work gets too challenging or the boss is cranky, but it's hard to persevere in the face of difficulty. Human beings just have a natural tendency to make excuses and quit. "I'm just not a science person." "I was never good at math." "I get tired very easily."

I hate to admit it, but I've said things like that from time to time too. Thinking this way creates a wall that holds back blessings in our lives. We'll never grow in areas where we only make excuses. We have to let diligence change us.

> The soul of the sluggard desireth, and hath nothing;
> But the soul of the diligent shall be made fat.
>
> Proverbs 13:4 ASV

It's interesting that the Bible uses the word *soul* in this verse. Your *soul* refers to your mind, your will, and your emotions.

Proverbs 13:4 tells us that it is the soul (emotions and feelings) that keep the lazy person from ever having anything of value. The problem isn't their circumstances. It's their soul.

If I were to rephrase that verse, here's what I believe it's saying: *People who give in to their feelings and emotions don't do well financially.*

All feelings aren't bad, but your feelings don't always line up with God's Word. You can't let your emotions be in the driver's seat of your life. You need them in the car. You need to have empathy. You need to love people, but you can't let your feelings dictate all your actions. Feelings will usually trade long-term satisfaction for short-term happiness. They'll sabotage the big things God wants to do in your life so you can feel good in the moment. You can't depend on your feelings because they don't always cooperate with God's ways. They don't consider the big picture. They only focus on the here and now. No matter how you feel about things, you have to let diligence and character rule your actions.

4. Diligence gives you influence.

The most important skill you can master is to do a job well even when you don't feel like doing it because diligence will give you influence.

> Diligent hands will rule...
>
> Proverbs 12:24 NIV

Our world doesn't need more stuff. It needs better leaders. We need people who understand God's ways and have influence.

Have you ever been somewhere and said, "Man, if I was the boss here, I would change that"? Every time I go into the post office or the DMV, I say under my breath, "I should go into politics. If I was in charge, I would change this."

God has called you to change things in your world. God has called you to listen to His voice. He's called me to be nice in the post office, but He may call you to work there and change it. As we learn and apply God's wisdom, He will show us how to do our jobs better.

Do you know how easy it is to get promoted in the world today? In most places the boss is looking for someone who can just show up on time and do a good job. It's almost that easy to get promoted, because that's what most people won't do. They won't show up on time or do a good job. If you're diligent, God wants to give you influence to change the things that bother you. No matter how many followers you have, Facebook can't do that. You can gripe about things all you want on social media, but nothing is going to change. God uses influencers who are filled with the power of His wisdom and are diligent to change the world.

5. Diligence teaches you how to be a godly leader.

> Jesus called them together and said, "You know that those who are regarded as rulers of the Gentiles lord it over them, and their high officials exercise authority over them. Not so with you. Instead, whoever wants to become great among you must be your servant, and whoever wants to be first must be slave of all. For even the Son of Man did not come to be served, but to serve, and to give his life as a ransom for many."
>
> Mark 10:42–45 NIV

In the world there are people who don't know God, and they just want to be the boss. But that's not God's way. Jesus said, "I went and did what I want you to do. I didn't just tell you about it; I showed you. Your influence is to be used and wielded differently." Our desire for leadership should be rooted in a heart to help and to serve people because that's what Jesus did.

Diligence gives us influence to lead in the same way that Jesus led. It's not about power. It's about serving others. Diligence isn't about self-gratification. It's about working hard and smart to gain influence in people's lives and help them to see Jesus in our lives. **God's blessings flow to the diligent leader who uses his or her place of influence as a witness for His kingdom.**

Diligence always levels the playing field. If you've ever looked at your situation and said, "That's not fair!" Be diligent, and sooner or later you'll get a chance to fix it. **Diligence is the great equalizer.**

There are some things that won't work. Maybe you made some risky investments and those didn't work. Maybe you thought the one-armed bandit or a get-rich-quick scheme was going to answer all of your problems, but it didn't work. Maybe nothing has worked, and you're frustrated. You're crying out to God, "I'm sick of being broke. I'm tired of not being able to bless my family. I want to be able to say 'yes' when You call me to bless our church and to help other people. Lord, help me!"

Diligence will work for you. Diligence to act on God's wisdom will give you influence that won't just impact your current situation. It will create a lasting impact on your future.

To become *WISER*, we need to walk in diligence.

As we work diligently to obey God's instructions, we need to keep these truths in mind:

- » **Diligence is a learned behavior.**

- » **Wisdom and diligence are two sides of the same coin.**

- » **Diligence is about your character, not about your personality.**

- » **Diligence gives you influence.**

- » **Diligence teaches you how to be a godly leader.**

KEY THOUGHTS

» Diligence is a learned behavior.

» Wisdom and diligence are two sides of the same coin.

» Diligence is about your character, not about your personality.

» Diligence gives you influence.

» Diligence teaches you how to be a godly leader.

CHAPTER 2

DILIGENCE BUILDS

SMALL GROUP AND
DEVOTIONAL LESSONS

READ

In God's system, wisdom is His way of paying us back, but to get the value of wisdom in our lives, **wisdom must be converted.** Wisdom is converted into financial blessing through hard work (diligence). Unfortunately we aren't born into this world with diligence. It's something we must grow in. **Wisdom and diligence are two sides of the same coin.** You can't convert wisdom without diligence, and if you only work hard and not smart (using God's wisdom), you'll never get ahead.

Diligence is less about personality and the miraculous and more about sweat equity and character. Your talent and personality may open doors for you, but ultimately you will rise or fall to your ability to pair wisdom with good, old-fashioned hard work. Not only does diligence convert wisdom, but **diligence gives you influence.** This reward of influence continues to return dividends the older and wiser you become.

Not only does diligence give you influence, but the process of applying wisdom through hard work teaches you how to hold onto what God wants to give you in the future. So many people want more, but if God actually gave them more, they wouldn't have the character to keep it. The process of building diligence sets you up to be able to do more with your life for God's glory. **Diligence teaches you how to become a godly leader.**

☐ **DAY 1**   **Proverbs 8 and 1 Samuel 8**

☐ **DAY 2**   **Proverbs 9 and 1 Samuel 9**

☐ **DAY 3**   **Proverbs 10 and 1 Samuel 10**

☐ **DAY 4**   **Proverbs 11 and 1 Samuel 11**

☐ **DAY 5**   **Proverbs 12 and 1 Samuel 12**

☐ **DAY 6**   **Proverbs 13 and 1 Samuel 13**

☐ **DAY 7**   **Proverbs 14 and 1 Samuel 14**

○○○○○ REFLECT ○○○○○

1. How do you get the most out of wisdom? What are the long-term benefits of diligence?

2. Has there been a time in your life when you knew what to do but a lack of diligence held you back? What did you learn from that experience?

○○○○○ WRITE ○○○○○

Journal your thoughts from the discussion questions here.

CHAPTER NOTES

CHAPTER 3

HONOR PROTECTS

If you were to ask the average person on the street what the keys to financial success are, you probably wouldn't get much push back at the suggestion that wisdom and diligence play a significant role. Although one subtle difference between God's formula for success and the world's is that the world tends to value education for education's sake and doesn't really understand the principles of God-given wisdom. Still, the world acknowledges working smart and working hard as pillars for building financial wealth. But the world is missing a key ingredient in their recipe for success that only people with a God-given revelation in the form of wisdom can understand.

Maybe you've never considered this before, but there are three primary reasons why many people struggle financially.

» **The first reason is that some are foolish.** They lack wisdom. We've all been around someone who was foolish with their money. It's foolish to spend more than you make. It's foolish to mortgage your future for a quick fix of happiness that will be gone a few moments after you make an impulse buy of another thing you don't really need. The old adage, "A fool and his money are soon parted," is the truth. The fool lacks wisdom, and true wealth will never be his.

» **Another reason some people end up broke is because they're lazy.** They lack diligence. Human beings are not born diligent. You can't just wish upon a star and have money fall from the sky into your lap. You have to be industrious and get after it if you're going to be successful in life. The problem is that it's hard to get up and work and push through when you don't feel like doing it. That's why many people quit early and don't stick around long enough to reap the rewards of diligence.

» **The third reason a lot of people end up broke is because they have a sense of entitlement.** Few people really understand how an attitude of entitlement holds them back. They believe they deserve to have every benefit in life regardless of their lack of wisdom and failure to be diligent in obtaining it. This is the missing ingredient in the world's recipe for success. They just don't get it. And it's what separates the people with true wealth from the people who just have a pile of money.

HONOR DIRECTLY AFFECTS YOUR WALLET

Wisdom, diligence, and honor go together, and honor serves as the base of success. Think of these three things as if they were the three sides of a triangle. If you take away one of these things, the other two would fall in on themselves. Wisdom and diligence are incomplete without honor.

We've looked at the principles of wisdom and diligence in the last two chapters, but now we need to look at the principles surrounding honor because a lack of honor directly affects your wallet. If you prefer, instead of the side of a triangle or the leg of a stool, you can think of honor as the flour in your pancakes. If you like big, fluffy pancakes, you can't leave out the flour. If you want a big, fluffy bank account, you can't skip the honor.

Honor is the glue that holds the other ingredients of financial success together, so it's important that we understand how it works.

1.   Honor is the foundation of every meaningful relationship.

Your destiny is tied to your relationships. You can never be successful financially (or any other way) apart from the relationships that God brings into your life. Without mutual honor, any relationship is doomed to fail.

If I want to have a great relationship with my wife, Kyla, I can't just tell her that I love her. I need to honor her. I need to show her respect and treat her as if she is important to me. If we're going to have peace in our home, I need to make sure that my kids honor her as well. If I ever begin to act as if Kyla owes me something or she is my servant, I can tell you that it wouldn't bode well for our relationship.

A few days ago, I had a lot of things going on at the church, and Kyla came home early and prepared us an awesome dinner. Kyla is usually very busy at work, so anytime we can sit down around the table at a family meal together, that's a very important time. I had given Kyla a time I would be home to enjoy the meal she prepared, but it seems like something always comes up around the end of the workday for me. Sure enough, just as I was about to leave the office, I got an urgent phone call about something I had to handle right away.

My first thought, because I've practiced honor with my wife, was to immediately call her and let her know. "Hey, Honey.

I'm going to be just a little bit late. Can we push dinner back a little bit?" Why did I call her? I did it because I wanted to honor her. Not letting her know I was going to be late would dishonor our relationship. (I also didn't want to die. Haha!)

I could say I loved Kyla all I wanted, but if I didn't honor her with my actions, my words would mean nothing. Honor works that way in every single relationship in your life.

If you're going to be successful in your financial life, you need to build relationships. Honor is huge in relationship building. You have to learn how to honor people.

Honor doesn't come naturally. Just as diligence is learned, honor is a part of our character that we must develop as well. The attitude of entitlement is natural to every human being born on this planet. From the womb, we grow up thinking someone owes us 24/7 care and our next meal. Operating in honor is a choice not a reflex.

2. **Honor is the foundation of our relationship with God.**

    Just as we have to honor people with whom we are in relationship, honor is the bedrock of a good relationship with God.

    You don't have to read very far into the Bible to find a story about a person or a group of people who started out honoring God, and when He gave them great blessings in return, they forgot about Him and stopped honoring God. As a result, all kinds of chaos came into their lives. When they got distracted by their wealth and possessions, their lack of honor brought about their demise.

    This doesn't just happen to worldly people. It happens to believers all the time. There's a story in the book of First Samuel about two priests, Phineas and Hophni, that will help us understand how honor is the foundation of our relationship with God.

Eli, the high priest of the nation of Israel, was their father, and Phineas and Hophni were overseers in the Tabernacle of God. But Phineas and Hophni didn't have any respect for God. They started using their jobs at the Tabernacle to take advantage of people. Phineas and Hophni took whatever they wanted from the people, whenever they wanted it. And because of their attitude of entitlement and dishonor for God's house, the people become angry and started to turn away from God.

It's a tragedy when people come into a church and see a bunch of people who are giving lip service to God but who aren't actually honoring His Word. Entitled, judgmental hypocrites turn people away from God every day. (Please, let's not let that be said about us!)

That's what was happening back in Israel. Phineas and Hophni were causing all kinds of problems. Not only were they taking the best parts of people's sacrifices for themselves, when women would come to the Tabernacle to serve and give their sacrifices, these two wicked men would manipulate them into having sex with them right there inside the Temple. They had no respect for God or humanity.

The worst part of the story is that their father, the high priest, knew what they were doing. Instead of disciplining his boys and standing up to them, Eli would just say something along the lines of, "Hey boys, y'all need to knock that off." But from a lifetime of passivity from Eli, Phineas and Hophni weren't about to stop their wicked behavior. All they ever got from Eli was lip service without any action. (In Texas, we would say Eli was "all hat and no cattle.") Eli was all bark and no bite. They knew that their father would never do anything to stop their evil behavior.

God warned Eli to take action, but the root of the problem was that Eli didn't really honor God either. He valued his sons above God's anointing, and in the end, it cost Eli everything.

"Why do you scorn my sacrifice and offering that I prescribed for my dwelling? Why do you honor your sons more than me by fattening yourselves on the choice parts of every offering made by my people Israel? Therefore the Lord, the God of Israel declares: 'I promised that members of your family would minister before me forever.' But now the Lord declares: 'Far be it from me! Those who honor me, I will honor, but those who despise me will be disdained.'"

1 Samuel 2:29–30 NIV

Honor is a big deal to God.

God had had enough disrespect and dishonor in His house, and He bypassed Eli to speak to another one of His servants who did understand the principle of honor. After that time, God began to speak to a young boy named Samuel.

3. Honor is a matter of the heart.

Honor comes from inside us. Honor originates from our hearts. To honor someone or not to honor them is a choice. Much like choosing to obey God's wisdom and choosing to be diligent in our work, honor doesn't come naturally to any of us. We all woke up this morning thinking about ourselves. *What am I going to get done today? What part of my body hurts? Who has offended me that I need to think about today?* From morning till night, we all just naturally think about ourselves.

We have to choose to prefer someone above ourselves.

These people honor me with their lips, but their hearts are far from me.

Matthew 15:8 NIV

Jesus is saying that if honor is just talk, it's not honor at all. It's actually dishonor. Honor isn't complete until our actions follow our words. I'm not talking about perfection. I'm not talking about being legalistic. I'm saying that our actions should be aligned with our words.

God wants to be respected by those who say they follow Him. To be successful in life, we need to be able to receive from God, and God will not bless those who refuse to honor Him.

4. Honor reminds us that we are stewards, not owners.

The word *steward* simply means manager. Everything from Heaven is delegated authority. We're not owners of the resources we have. As a pastor of a church in a military town, I can tell you that people who have been in the military understand how this principle works. You don't obey your commander because they're perfect or because they have told you to do the right thing. You do what they tell you to do because of the authority they represent in your chain of command.

The principle of honor for authority reminds us that we're managers, not owners. In the Bible, this is the principle of *stewardship.* It's dangerous when we consider everything we have as our own.

> And he [Jesus] told them this parable: "The ground of a certain rich man yielded an abundant harvest. He thought to himself, 'What shall I do? I have no place to store my crops.' Then he said, 'This is what I will do. I will tear down my barns and build bigger ones, and there I will store my surplus grain. And I'll say to myself, 'You have plenty of grain laid up for many years. Take life easy; eat, drink and be merry.' But God said to him, 'You fool! This very night your life will be demanded from you. Then who will get what you prepared for yourself?' This is how it will be with whoever stores up things for themselves but is not rich toward God."

Luke 12:16–21 NIV

You and I are only stewards. We're caretakers of what's been given to us. We came into this world with nothing, and we're all going to leave with nothing. Our stuff is not our stuff. We only have it because God has been gracious to us. This is a strong statement, but everything we have above the level of Hell is from God's grace. Some of us may only have a little right now, and some of us may have much. But, we're all managers or stewards.

The man in this story in the book of Luke was not rich toward God because his heart was far from God. He didn't understand honor.

5. **Honor without a test is only lip service.**

If you're a normal parent, you probably love to give good gifts to your kids. The Bible says you don't even have to be a good person for that to be enjoyable. Good and bad people alike love giving good gifts to their kids. Kyla and I love giving good gifts to our children too, but every now and then, we also create a little test for them. "Sure darling, you can keep looking at your iPhone, which I paid for, which I supply the Internet service for, which I paid for all the apps on—but first, you have to clean your room."

We give our children tests all the time because we know that one thing the world will not tolerate is ungrateful children. You know the kids I'm talking about. Don't you hate to see a child in a store or a restaurant who is throwing a tantrum about something they wanted that they didn't get?

Kyla and I don't want our children to ever be ungrateful, so testing their understanding every now and again is a way that we can make sure they realize they're only stewards of all the good things we've provided for them. (If you're a parent, for the love of everyone else in the world, *PLEASE* teach your children this principle. If you don't, they're going to be entitled, spiritual babies when they grow up because they never learned how to be grateful.)

We don't test our children to assert some kind of dominance over them. We do it to make sure that they don't love *the gift* more than *the giver*. We want to remind our kids that what you have really isn't yours. It was all given to you by the wonderful, powerful grace of Mom and Dad.

If you pause for a moment and think about it, God is a parent too. He's a much better parent than you and I are. God loves to give good gifts to His kids, but along the way, He also uses tests to check our hearts. He wants to find out, "Do they love Me because I give them stuff, or do they love Me because they love Me?"

Honor without a test is only lip service. We see the first one of these tests in the Bible.

> And the Lord God commanded the man, "You are free to eat from any tree in the garden; but you must not eat from the tree of the knowledge of good and evil, for when you eat from it you will certainly die."
>
> Genesis 2:16–17 NIV

It's interesting that God didn't put a fence around the tree, and He didn't put it in some obscure place where Adam and Eve would never see it. That tree was planted in the center of the Garden of Eden, where every time the man looked into the garden, he would have a choice. *Am I going to honor God, or am I going to dishonor Him and take something that's not mine?* God isn't interested in having robots serve Him. He doesn't want our relationship with Him to be one without free will. You can't really honor God without the ability to dishonor Him if you so choose. And just as it was in the time of Adam and Eve, one of the greatest areas where we can show God that we will choose to honor Him is in the area of our money and possessions.

> For where your treasure is, there your heart will be also.
>
> Matthew 6:21 NIV

Jesus said that there's an invisible string that can tie our hearts to our stuff. But this attachment to money and possessions can never truly fulfill the desires God created your heart to long for. The satisfaction that comes from material possessions may linger for a moment, but in the end, you'll always come up short. Only a deep and honoring relationship with God can bring lasting peace and joy to your soul.

ONE SIMPLE TEST

Do we really love God, or do we only love the blessings He provides? There's a simple way to find out. God laid out a test in Scripture that will show us the truth.

Honoring God begins with the tithe.

God asks us for the first ten percent of all of our increase to make sure that our heartstrings are firmly attached to Him and never get attached to our money.

I realize that most times when you hear about tithing it's taught from a perspective of giving, but that's really not the purpose of the tithe. Also, although your tithe is certainly a blessing to your local church, supporting the church financially isn't the primary purpose of the tithe either.

Remember, the principles of the economy of God are not just about giving because if you don't understand how to receive from God, you'll never be able to give. Many good, Christian people are held back financially in life because they have an unhealthy, ungodly attachment to their stuff. The command from God to tithe is the test that removes that bond.

"I the Lord do not change. So you, the descendants of Jacob, are not destroyed. Ever since the time of your ancestors you have turned away from my decrees and have not kept them. Return to me, and I will return to you," says the Lord Almighty. "But you ask, 'How are we to return?' Will a mere mortal rob God? Yet you rob me. But you ask, 'How are we robbing you?' In tithes and offerings. You are under a curse—your whole nation—because you are robbing me. Bring the whole tithe into the storehouse, that there may be food in my house. Test me in this," says the Lord Almighty, "and see if I will not throw open the floodgates of heaven and pour out so much blessing that there will not be room enough to store it. I will prevent pests from devouring your crops, and the vines in your fields will not drop their fruit before it is ripe," says the Lord Almighty. "Then all the nations will call you blessed, for yours will be a delightful land," says the Lord Almighty.

Malachi 3:6–12 NIV

Did you notice how the passage about God's test of the tithe begins? "I the Lord do not change." I find that statement fascinating because many people would say, "Well, tithing isn't for today. That was the Old Testament." I think God wanted to help us with that, so He started out by saying, "I the Lord do not change." Tithing is still God's test of honor. It has always been His test, and it will always be His test. Aren't you glad God was clear in His instructions? He goes on to say that the test was for, "You, the descendants of Jacob," which is actually all of us.

And then God told His people that they weren't passing the test. The people were blessed, but they started dishonoring God. They started pulling away from Him. They realized that as they got farther away from God, He got farther from them. They knew that only one thing could satisfy the deep desires of their hearts, and they cried out. "God, we want You back." And God told them that, if they would draw near to Him, He would reestablish His relationship with them.

God, in His infinite grace, took time to explain why things hadn't been going well for them in the past. He told His people they were under a curse because the nation was robbing Him in their tithes and offerings.

Before I go any further, I do want to make note of a side item here. A lot of people mis-teach this section of Scripture. It's not God who curses people. That's not what God does or who He is. God was only pointing out the obvious. The people were under a curse that they had brought upon themselves by depending upon the world's system to satisfy their needs.

In the world's system, the devourer is free to kill, steal, and destroy you and your stuff. Have you ever noticed how your car never breaks down when you have the money to fix it? Have you noticed that unexpected need only feels unexpected because you don't have the resources to deal with it? That's the curse of this world's system. Have you felt the pull for your hard-earned money from everyone around you? That's the way the world works. The world takes away from one to give to another. The bad news is that our money and possessions are already under a curse because we all live in the world.

Fortunately, there is a way to break the curse of the world's economy off of your finances. It's found in God's promise given to those who pass His test.

> "Bring the whole tithe into the storehouse, that there may be food in my house. Test me in this," says the Lord Almighty, "and see if I will not throw open the floodgates of heaven and pour out so much blessing that there will not be room enough to store it. I will prevent pests from devouring your crops, and the vines in your fields will not drop their fruit before it is ripe," says the Lord Almighty.
>
> Malachi 3:10–11 NIV

There's the test—*bringing the whole tithe into the storehouse (your local church).* **And here's the promise**—*open windows of wisdom that will bring so much blessing there won't be room to contain it, and the devourer will be stopped from taking it away!* What a promise! God wants to bless us! The tithe is for our good! God isn't looking for our money, He's looking for our hearts.

The tithe is simply a test to show that you're going to honor God and His way of living instead of trusting the world's system to meet your needs. A Christian who doesn't tithe doesn't honor God. You can have all the wisdom and work really hard, but if you don't honor God and pass the tithe test, you will never get ahead. Your wealth will not last because the devourer will continually pull you back.

The Lord will never ask you to do something that takes away from or diminishes you. He only asks you to do things that build you up and protect you. If you're struggling with honoring God in the tithe, I pray that God will give you the faith to trust Him at His Word. You don't need to suffer in guilt, condemnation, or shame over the past. That's not how God operates. He's simply asking you to trust Him now and honor Him with the tithe.

As we diligently act on the wisdom God gives us, honoring God will bring us lasting wealth. Let's remember these principles about honor.

- » **Honor is the foundation of every meaningful relationship.**

- » **Honor is the foundation of our relationship with God.**

- » **Honor is a matter of the heart.**

- » **Honor reminds us that we are stewards, not owners.**

- » **Honor without a test is only lip service.**

- » **Honoring God begins with the tithe.**

KEY THOUGHTS

» Honor is the foundation of every meaningful relationship.

» Honor is the foundation of our relationship with God.

» Honor is a matter of the heart.

» Honor reminds us that we are stewards, not owners.

» Honor without a test is only lip service.

» Honoring God begins with the tithe.

CHAPTER 3

HONOR PROTECTS

SMALL GROUP AND DEVOTIONAL LESSONS

✪✪✪✪✪ READ ✪✪✪✪✪

Wisdom is the currency of God's system, and diligence (hard work) is what converts God's wisdom into financial blessing. None of this matters if what we're building isn't protected by honor. Honor serves as an umbrella over our lives. When we trust God and His ways, He promises to protect what we're building. **Honor is the foundation of our relationship with God.** Wisdom, diligence, and honor go together, and honor serves as the base (the foundation) of how we build and steward wealth God's way.

To honor someone is a choice. Much like choosing to obey God's wisdom and choosing to be diligent in our work, honor doesn't come naturally to any of us. **Honor is a matter of the heart.**

God wants to be respected by those who say they follow Him. To be successful in life, we need to be able to receive from God, and God will not bless those who refuse to honor Him. **Honor reminds us that we are managers, not owners.** In the Bible, this is the principle of *stewardship*. It's dangerous when we believe that everything we have is our own. Do we really love God, or do we only love the blessings He provides? There's a simple way to find out. God laid out a test in Scripture to reveal the truth. **Honoring God begins with the tithe.**

☐ **DAY 1**   **Proverbs 15 and 1 Samuel 15**

☐ **DAY 2**   **Proverbs 16 and 1 Samuel 16**

☐ **DAY 3**   **Proverbs 17 and 1 Samuel 17**

☐ **DAY 4**   **Proverbs 18 and 1 Samuel 18**

☐ **DAY 5**   **Proverbs 19 and 1 Samuel 19**

☐ **DAY 6**   **Proverbs 20 and 1 Samuel 20**

☐ **DAY 7**   **Proverbs 21 and 1 Samuel 21**

○○○○○ REFLECT ○○○○○

1. What is honor, and where does it come from?

2. Why does it seem so difficult to honor God with our financial resources? What is stewardship, and why is having the perspective of being a steward important in how we live our lives?

○○○○○ WRITE ○○○○○

Journal your thoughts from the discussion questions here.

_____

_____

_____

_____

_____

_____

_____

_____

_____

_____

_____

_____

_____

_____

_____

_____

_____

CHAPTER NOTES

CHAPTER 4

FAITH OVERCOMES

Have you ever taken a test? Maybe it was a midterm to finally complete a dreaded class in school. (For me that class was always math or science.) Where I live, the effectiveness of standardized tests is widely debated, as educators argue about the best way to measure someone's knowledge of different subjects.

I've always been fascinated with I.Q. (Intelligence Quotient) tests. Consisting of a number of questions measuring various components of intelligence, including short-term memory, analytical thinking, mathematical ability, spacial recognition, and more, these tests don't just measure your knowledge. They measure your capacity to learn or your intelligence quotient. In other words, I.Q. tests measure potential. Social scientists have also created similar tests that measure your E.Q. (Emotional Quotient) to determine your potential to build strong and healthy relationships with others.

So, what does this have to do with resources and building wealth? Well, there is a test in the Bible that's similar to these tests, in that it predicts your potential to succeed in God's economy. It's called the test of faith. Your F.Q. (Faith Quotient) determines your potential to overcome the inevitable delays and setbacks of life.

I.Q.	E.Q.	F.Q.
Intelligence Quotient	**Emotional Quotient**	**Faith Quotient**
(intelligence potential, knowledge)	**(potential for strong, healthy relationships)**	**(potential to overcome delays and setbacks)**

Jesus said this about the world:

> I have told you all this so that you may have peace in
> me. Here on earth you will have many trials and sorrows.
> But take heart, because I have overcome the world.
>
> John 16:33 NLT

Faith allows us to overcome adversity and to take hold of the promises given to us by God through Jesus' sacrifice on the cross and by the power of His resurrection. As we wrap up the four principles for becoming **WISER** with our resources, I want to uncover one final principle—the principle of overcoming faith.

When you hear the word faith, depending on your religious background or lack thereof, your mind probably flashes to several thoughts or ideas. Early in my relationship with God, I struggled to overcome doubt and fear. I remember someone at church just telling me to "push through" and to have faith. When I asked them what that meant, they couldn't really give me a clear answer. Their answers seemed vague and mysterious. Many of their answers seemed to involve some mystical feeling of closeness to God which only happened after you prayed for hours or "totally surrendered" in a worship service.

As I began to grow and learn more about God from the Bible, I realized that faith is not a feeling, but it is absolutely essential to our relationship with God. As Christians, it is critical that we understand what faith is for one very important reason.

We cannot please God without faith.

> But without faith it is impossible to please Him, for
> he who comes to God must believe that He is, and that
> He is a rewarder of those who diligently seek Him.
>
> Hebrews 11:6 NKJV

I love this verse because it emphasizes the importance of faith. The author of Hebrews gets right to the heart of the issue by examining what we believe about God. Many people see God as some cosmic killjoy looking to take our fun away or some all-powerful, mythological, Zeus-like figure who is just waiting for us to step out of line so He can zap us with a lightning bolt. When you look at the character of God throughout Scripture, however, you see that nothing could be farther from the truth.

Hebrews 11:6 says that the reason it is impossible to please God without faith is because we must believe that He is good and that He is a rewarder of those who seek Him or those who build and steward according to His ways.

GOD IS A GOOD FATHER

So if you sinful people know how to give good gifts to your children, how much more will your heavenly Father give good gifts to those who ask him.

Matthew 7:11 NLT

God is first and foremost our Father. What does a healthy father want for his children? If I'm being honest, I really didn't understand the answer to that question until I became a father. I remember being in the delivery room when our first child, Adilyn, was born. I was absolutely terrified. Sure, I looked calm and collected on the outside, but inside I was a wreck. I can't explain the intensity of my feelings except to say that, in that room, at that moment, all I wanted was for my baby girl to be happy and healthy. My desires for her have evolved since that day. I still want her to be happy and healthy, but I also want her to keep her room clean! My point is that if I want health and happiness for my daughter, I can't imagine how much greater God's love and desire is for us as His children.

Faith in God's love for His children corresponds to the core of how we build and steward wealth. Faith is all about believing that God is good and that He rewards us as we put Him first and operate within His guidelines. This belief helps us in every area of our lives, including our marriages, our families, our friendships, our health, and our finances. Because faith is essential, I think it's important that we understand a few of its characteristics:

1. **Faith is based on reality—the reality of God's truth.**

   > Now faith is the substance of things hoped for, the evidence of things not seen.
   >
   > Hebrews 11:1 NKJV

   Faith is substance. It isn't blind. God never asks us to believe blindly. The great thing about God is that He never asks us to take leaps; He asks us to take steps. As we take one step in faith, our confidence grows, and it becomes easier to take the next step.

2. **We grow in faith from hearing God's Word.**

   > So then faith comes by hearing, and hearing by the word of God.
   >
   > Romans 10:17 NKJV

   We know who God is and how He operates by knowing His Word, the Bible. God will never contradict or alter His Word to accommodate our circumstances. In other words, our lives orbit around God and His Word; He doesn't orbit around us and our opinions or experiences.

3. **Faith releases the power of God to change our lives and our circumstances.**

   > He replied, "Because you have so little faith. Truly I tell you, if you have faith as small as a mustard seed, you can say to this mountain, 'Move from here to there,' and it will move. Nothing will be impossible for you."
   >
   > Matthew 17:20 NIV

   It is important for us to understand that faith isn't just some mystical feeling. Faith is given to us to get things done. As we're building and stewarding what God has given us, there will be times when we'll need faith to receive what God has for us. The good news is that a little faith goes a long way. We need it to take hold of God's promises.

WHERE DOES FAITH COME FROM?

When people receive the truth of the Gospel and accept Jesus as their Lord, there is something very special that happens on the inside of them.

> For I say, through the grace given to me, to everyone who is among you, not to think of himself more highly than he ought to think, but to think soberly, as God has dealt to each one a measure of faith.
>
> Romans 12:3 NKJV

> For by grace you have been saved through faith, and that not of yourselves; it is the gift of God, not of works, lest anyone should boast.
>
> Ephesians 2:8–9 NKJV

Supernatural, biblical faith is a gift that is given to us when we call on the name of Jesus Christ. At the point of salvation, God gives every believer the same measure of faith. God is no respecter of persons. He doesn't give more faith to one and less faith to another.

Yet, it is obvious that some Christians walk in a greater faith than others. How can this be so?

The explanation is simple. **Faith can grow.**

> We ought to always thank God always for you, brothers and sisters, and rightly so, **because your faith is growing more and more,** and the love all of you have for one another is increasing.
>
> 2 Thessalonians 1:3 NIV, Author's emphasis

Saving faith is a changing faith. When you accept Christ as your Lord and Savior, your heart (your spirit) is renewed (regenerated) on the inside.

> This means that anyone who belongs to Christ has become a new person. The old life is gone; a new life has begun!
>
> 2 Corinthians 5:17 NLT

When you are born again, you receive the gift of saving faith. God's miracle-working power changes the old spirit inside of you (full of sinful desires and lusts), and your spirit is recreated to become a new creation (with God's righteousness) in Christ Jesus.

But that's not the end. It's up to you to increase your faith by hearing and hearing the Word of God (Romans 10:17). As you grow in faith and put your trust in the truth of God's Word, a growing, overcoming faith begins to help you grasp the unseen and walk in a belief that brings God's power into your life in other areas besides salvation. Just as saving faith changes your spirit and makes it new, overcoming faith releases the miraculous power of God to change your life and your circumstances.

The Apostle John explains it this way.

> For everyone born of God overcomes the world. This is the victory that has overcome the world, even our faith.
>
> 1 John 5:4 NIV

In other words, **overcoming faith is faith that gives you the victory to overcome the world.** Faith in God and His Word is the spiritual bulldozer that moves the mountains that try to block the road to your destiny, your resources, and your victory.

Your circumstances may seem immovable, unchangeable, or impossible. Maybe you suffered a failure, an offense, a medical situation, or a financial breakdown in your past that seems insurmountable. Your problem may just be sitting there blocking your way.

Faith gives you the confidence to stand and face the problem head on, even when the situation may seem impossible. Faith is the assurance that God is working on your behalf according to His Word and that your mountain will have to get out of the way!

> Now faith is confidence in what we hope for and assurance about what we do not see.
>
> Hebrews 11:1 NIV

Let's look at that verse in the Amplified Bible.

> Now faith is the assurance (title deed, confirmation) of things hoped for (divinely guaranteed), and the evidence of things not seen [the conviction of their reality—faith comprehends as fact what cannot be experienced by the physical senses].
>
> Hebrews 11:1 AMP

In the Greek, the illustration of this principle is related to how a title deed works. If I have the finances to do so, I can buy a house that I have never seen in another state where I've never been. If I have the title deed to the property, I own that house whether or not I've ever set foot inside of it. The title deed is my confirmation that the house belongs to me. It is mine.

Faith is holding the title to all that God has for you—before it even manifests. Faith is the title—the guaranteed confirmation and proof—that what God has promised you is already a reality in the spirit realm. You may not see it in this physical world yet, but you can be absolutely sure that what God has promised will come to pass.

Hebrews 11:1 tells us that hope is important. Hope lets you see the possibility that what God has promised could become a reality for you some time off in the future, but faith gives you the confidence to stand and believe that God's promises are yours today. **Faith gives you the confidence to stand when the circumstances that surround you seem impossible.**

That doesn't mean you won't face any challenges or problems along the way to receiving what God has promised you. The enemy of your faith, the devil, will not just let you cruise by uncontested. You will need to stand strong in faith until God's promises are manifested in your life.

> That you do not become sluggish, but imitate those who through faith and patience inherit the promises.
>
> Hebrews 6:12 NKJV

Hold tight to that deed for a godly family, even when your family may look like a wreck. Stand strong in faith, believing for that wayward child, when you know God has an amazing call on his or her life. Rest securely in the Word of God, and believe for a breakthrough in the area of your finances.

God has promised to supply all your needs according to His riches in glory by Christ Jesus (Philippians 4:19). He has given you all things that pertain to life and godliness (2 Peter 1:3). God is a rewarder of those who diligently seek Him (Hebrews 11:6). Even if your resources haven't been abundant, you have the title deed to receive those promises from your wonderful, loving, Heavenly Father. You may not see it in the natural yet, but your faith will bring what you see in your spirit into being in this natural world.

FAITH LIKE ABRAHAM

There's probably no greater example in the Bible of how faith worked in the life of a person than there is in the story of Abraham. God gave Abraham a picture of his future on the inside, and Abraham's faith and patience brought him the promise.

> And not being weak in faith, he did not consider his own body, already dead (since he was about a hundred years old), and the deadness of Sarah's womb. He did not waver at the promise of God through unbelief, but was strengthened in faith, giving glory to God.
>
> Romans 4:19–20 NKJV

If there's one word that we hear connected to Abraham, it's the word *faith*. God promised to multiply Abraham's family, and, as a result, his family would bless the whole world. What does Abraham's life demonstrate for us? I think if he could meet with us today, he would tell us this one thing: **"Trust God because He always keeps His promises."**

As we look at the life of Abraham, whom we call "The Father of Faith," we can see that he wasn't perfect. He had moments of doubt. God had told Abraham that he was going to be the father of many nations (Genesis 12:2), but as he was approaching age ninety, Abraham still didn't have a single child.

From Abraham's story, we can see some very important things about how faith works in our lives to bring God's power into our circumstances.

» **Faith is developed over time.** God promised that Abraham would be a father of nations, yet after many years Abraham and Sarah still didn't have a son. I'm going to let you in on a little secret about God that you may not want to hear. **God is never late, but He's rarely ever early.**

Even Abraham, the great Father of Faith, struggled with God's timing.

> Now Sarai, Abram's wife, had borne him no children. But she had an Egyptian slave named Hagar; so she said to Abram, "The Lord has kept me from having children. Go, sleep with my slave; perhaps I can build a family through her." Abram agreed to what Sarai said.
>
> Genesis 16:1–2 NIV

Abraham and Sarah did what we all do when we think God is taking too long. We try to make God's promise happen on our own. But when we take God's promise into our own hands, we always settle for less and create unnecessary delays and problems for ourselves.

We live in an "instant" society. We're used to getting what we want when we want it. We are a "right now" generation.

This is a hard truth, but our timing and God's timing are not always the same.

Abraham and Sarah decided to take matters into their own hands, and Ishmael was the result of their scheme. But God's plan was for Abraham to have a son through Sarah, and God came to Abraham in a vision to set Abraham back on the right path.

> Then the word of the Lord came to him: "This man will not be your heir, but a son who is your own flesh and blood will be your heir." He took him outside and said, "Look up at the sky and count the stars—if indeed you can count them." Then he said to him, "So shall your offspring be." Abraham believed the Lord, and he credited it to him as righteousness.
>
> Genesis 15:4–6 NIV

Abraham was discouraged, but when God spoke to him, he trusted God at His Word. Even though it looked as if God's plan would never come to pass in Abraham's life, Abraham believed God's Word, and he received the promise.

Biblical faith is trusting God to provide the answer to our problems and obeying Him in bringing it to pass.

» **Faith is built one step at a time.** God never calls you to move all at once. He always leads in stages or steps.

> Then the Lord appeared to Abram and said, "I will give this land to your descendants." And Abram built an altar there and dedicated it to the Lord, who had appeared to him. After that, Abram traveled south and set up camp in the hill country, with Bethel to the west and Ai to the east. There he built another altar and dedicated it to the Lord, and he worshiped the Lord.

Then Abram continued traveling south by stages toward the Negev.

Genesis 12:7–9 NLT

Often, we get so wrapped up with the ultimate outcome, but God is only asking us to take the step right in front of us.

And why do you worry about clothes? See how the flowers of the field grow. They do not labor or spin. Yet I tell you that not even Solomon in all his splendor was dressed like one of these. If that is how God clothes the grass of the field, which is here today and tomorrow is thrown into the fire, will he not much more clothe you— you of little faith? So do not worry, saying, "What shall we eat?" or "What shall we drink?" or "What shall we wear?" For the pagans run after all these things, and your heavenly Father knows that you need them. But seek first his kingdom and his righteousness, and all these things will be given to you as well. Therefore do not worry about tomorrow, for tomorrow will worry about itself. Each day has enough trouble of its own.

Matthew 6:28–34 NIV

When you don't know what to do, go back to what you know. Just take the next step in front of you. God leads us in steps, not in leaps.

OVERCOMING FAITH

So Jesus answered and said to them, "Have faith in God. For assuredly, I say to you, whoever says to this mountain, 'Be removed and be cast into the sea,' and does not doubt in his heart, but believes that those things he says will be done, he will have whatever he says. Therefore I say to you, whatever things you ask when you pray, believe that you receive them, and you will have them. And whenever you stand praying, if you have anything against anyone, forgive him, that your Father in heaven may also forgive you your trespasses. But if you do not forgive, neither will your Father in heaven forgive your trespasses."

Mark 11:22–26 NKJV

Jesus tells us that we can have mountain-moving, miracle-releasing faith, if we will remember these four important things.

1.   Faith is released through our mouths.

> For assuredly, I say to you, whoever says to this mountain, "Be removed and be cast into the sea," and does not doubt in his heart, but believes that those things he says will be done, he will have whatever he says.

Mark 11:23 NKJV

Think about this question: Did Jesus tell us to *PRAY* that the problem, obstacle, or mountain that looms before us would be removed? No, He said, "**SAY to the mountain** be removed, and be cast into the sea."

We often hear people say that prayer changes things. But that's not entirely true. **Prayer changes us. Faith changes things.** Jesus didn't say, "If you encounter a mountain, pray that it would go away." No, He said, "Have faith in God and then verbally, audibly, and with your mouth tell the mountain to be removed." When seemingly insurmountable hindrances block our paths, we must speak to those obstacles in faith for them to be removed.

Jesus spoke to numerous obstacles, but one of the most notable times was when Jesus was tempted directly by Satan. Three times, in three different ways, the devil tempted Jesus, and each time Jesus responded with, "It is written." (See Matthew 4:1–11.) Jesus came against His opposition with the Spoken Word of God, and the enemy had to move!

Here's one very important thing to note, though: Speaking *TO* your mountains is not the same thing as speaking *ABOUT* them. Faith remains God-focused, not problem-focused. Whatever you focus on will grow in your life. If you focus on speaking the truths and the promises in the Word of God, your faith will grow, and your circumstances will have to change. But if all you do is complain about your situation, things will inevitably get worse. Whatever comes out of your mouth repeatedly will become a self-fulfilling prophecy.

2. **We must believe God wants to answer our prayers.**

> Therefore I say to you, whatever things you ask when you pray, believe that you receive them, and you will have them.

>   Mark 11:24 NKJV

In this verse, Jesus commands us to believe that we have the answer at the moment when we ask God for something in prayer. Remember, faith is believing that we have the title deed to the things that we haven't seen as a reality in the natural realm yet.

Wait a minute! What?! Does that mean we can just pray for ANYTHING, and if we believe, we'll receive it?

That's a question that has divided members in the Body of Christ for years.

Some people preach a "prosperity gospel" where God just grants wishes like some magical genie in a bottle that we own. Others believe that God wants His children to go through great lack and suffering to become more holy through pain. I believe the truth rests in the middle.

Let's take a look at some other verses about receiving answers to our prayers.

> If you abide in Me, and My words abide in you, you will ask what you desire, and it shall be done for you.
>
> John 15:7 NKJV

> But let him ask in faith, with no doubting, for he who doubts is like a wave of the sea driven and tossed by the wind. For let not that man suppose that he will receive anything from the Lord; he is a double-minded man, unstable in all his ways.
>
> James 1:6–8 NKJV

I believe that the key to receiving the answer to our prayers is found in a word Jesus used in John 15:7. It's the word *abide*. In the Greek, that word means *to live, to dwell in, or to remain.*

The key to receiving the answer to our prayers lies in the source of biblical faith. **It's abiding in Jesus and His Word.**

Are we abiding in His Word? Are we doing what it says? If we aren't, then we can't expect blessings to follow us everywhere we go. But if we are living and abiding in Him to the best of our ability, (remember, nobody is perfect) then we can come boldly to Him and believe that He will grant what we have asked.

The Apostle John explains it this way:

> Now this is the confidence that we have in Him, that if we ask anything according to His will, He hears us. And if we know that He hears us, whatever we ask, we know that we have the petitions that we have asked of Him.
>
> 1 John 5:14–15 NKJV

According to these verses, we can have complete confidence and unwavering faith that anything we ask for **according to God's will,** will be granted. And the way we know we are asking according to God's will is that we are abiding in Jesus and in His Holy Word. The Bible is the written expression of God's will. Jesus, the Word of God made flesh, demonstrated for us that God unequivocally wants to bless His children. The promises God made to His children in the Bible apply to you and me. We can believe that, without a doubt.

Sorry, but you can't find a verse in the Bible saying that God wants you to win Powerball tomorrow, but you can find plenty of promises that God wants you to be saved, blessed, happy, and whole so that you can be a blessing and help lead others into His kingdom. You can put your faith in that.

3. The enemy of our faith is unforgiveness.

And whenever you stand praying, if you have anything against anyone, forgive him, that your Father in heaven may also forgive you your trespasses. But if you do not forgive, neither will your Father in heaven forgive your trespasses.

Mark 11:25–26 NKJV

There is one thing that we see that quickly fizzles our faith, and that's unforgiveness. Jesus clearly linked faith to walking in forgiveness. If we're harboring offense against another person it will quench our faith, and our prayers will go unanswered. Unforgiveness short-circuits the power of God in our circumstances and allows the enemy to hold us captive to offense.

Faith is a powerful force that can move the mountains that stand in our way, but we must not give the enemy a foothold through the sin of unforgiveness.

As we wrap up this chapter on faith, we come full circle on how God uses our faith to help us overcome in every way, but especially for our purposes in this book, in regard to our resources. Let's look back at the scripture verse we started with.

> But without faith it is impossible to please Him, for
> he who comes to God must believe that He is, and that
> He is a rewarder of those who diligently seek Him.
>
> Hebrews 11:6 NKJV

When we apply God's wisdom to our life and work diligently with what He has put into our hands, our faith overcomes what stands against us. And as our faith overcomes, a snowball effect happens. One day, we look up and realize that we lack no good thing, and what's even better is that we can see how we now have become a conduit of God's blessing for others. Faith grows in us as we continue to trust God's Word and His work in us.

> Good people leave an inheritance to their
> grandchildren, but the sinner's wealth passes to the
> godly.
>
> Proverbs 13:22 NLT

When we trust in God and His ways, God doesn't just bless us. He also blesses our children. How we steward and manage our resources has a direct effect on the legacy we leave behind for our children and grandchildren. As we overcome, we establish a foundation that future generations will build upon, ensuring that our work in this lifetime will outlive us.

As we spend time in God's Word and build up our faith in His promises, let's remember these principles about faith.

- » **We cannot please God without faith.**

- » **Faith is based on reality—the reality of God's truth.**

- » **We grow in faith by hearing God's Word.**

- » **Faith releases the power of God to change our lives and our circumstances.**

- » **Faith is developed over time**

- » **Faith is developed one step at a time.**

» **Faith is released through our mouths.**

» **We must believe God wants to answer our prayers.**

» **The enemy of our faith is unforgiveness.**

KEY THOUGHTS

» We cannot please God without faith.

» Faith is based on reality—the reality of God's truth.

» We grow in faith by hearing God's Word.

» Faith releases the power of God to change our lives and our circumstances.

» Faith is developed over time.

» Faith is developed one step at a time.

» Faith is released through our mouths.

» We must believe God wants to answer our prayers.

» The enemy of our faith is unforgiveness.

FAITH OVERCOMES

SMALL GROUP AND
DEVOTIONAL LESSONS

READ

It is critical that we understand what faith is because **without faith we cannot please God.** God is first and foremost a Father. And like any earthly dad, God is most pleased with us when we trust that He is a good Father who loves to give good gifts to His children.

This faith in God isn't just a feeling. **Faith is based on reality—the reality of God's truth.** As we continue to get to know God through the Bible and begin to obey it, our faith increases. **Faith is developed over time.** It is a process of trusting God at His Word and moving from information to transformation in our lives. As we mature in our relationships with God, our faith grows because of our experience of God's goodness.

Because God has been so good to us, our F.Q. (Faith Quotient) is connected to our ability to forgive others who do us wrong. God gave His Son, Jesus, as the ultimate sacrifice for our sin so that we could be forgiven. He expects us to pay forward this forgiveness to those who wrong us. **The enemy of our faith is unforgiveness.**

When we trust God, He doesn't just bless us. He also blesses our children and their children. Faith is the great multiplier in our lives. As we grow, we need faith to overcome the inevitable setbacks and failures we will encounter on the way to becoming who God's created us to be. **Faith releases the power of God to change our lives and circumstances.**

- -

☐ **DAY 1**   **Proverbs 22 and 1 Samuel 22**

☐ **DAY 2**   **Proverbs 23 and 1 Samuel 23**

☐ **DAY 3**   **Proverbs 24 and 1 Samuel 24**

☐ **DAY 4**   **Proverbs 25 and 1 Samuel 25**

☐ **DAY 5**   **Proverbs 26 and 1 Samuel 26**

☐ **DAY 6**   **Proverbs 27 and 1 Samuel 27**

☐ **DAY 7**   **Proverbs 28 and 1 Samuel 28**

○○○○○ REFLECT ○○○○○

1. What is faith, and why is it so important to have?

2. Is your faith growing? Why or why not? If you believe your faith is not growing, what are some ways you could put yourself back on track?

○○○○○ WRITE ○○○○○

Journal your thoughts from the discussion questions here.

_____

_____

_____

_____

_____

_____

_____

_____

_____

_____

_____

_____

_____

_____

CHAPTER NOTES

SECTION 2

THE PRACTICALS

The next four chapters will help you practically apply each of the four principles to your life today. They provide a starting point to build and to steward your life and resources God's way.

SECTION NOTES

CHAPTER 5

A WISE PLAN

Think back to when you were a child. Did you hope that one day you'd be rich? I certainly did. When I was growing up, I used to think that if I were rich, money would solve all of my problems. But if being rich solves problems, shouldn't Hollywood be the happiest place on Earth? That's not what we see in the news. A lot of those rich and famous movie stars are addicted to drugs or alcohol, get in knock-down-drag-out fights at the clubs, and have terrible family lives. Hollywood is not a very happy place, and money is not the answer to the world's problems.

> Command those who are rich in this present world
> not to be arrogant nor to put their hope in wealth, which
> is so uncertain, but to put their hope in God, who richly
> provides us with everything for our enjoyment.
>
> 1 Timothy 6:17 NIV

As we saw in the last chapter, when people put their hope in their wealth, it doesn't turn out so well. The Apostle Paul warns those who are rich in this world not to put their trust in God because the world's wealth is uncertain and can't be trusted.

You might say to me, "Well, Pastor, that verse doesn't apply to me because I'm not rich," but that's where you're wrong.

The definition of *rich* is a moving target. In a recent Gallup Poll, pollsters asked people who were making approximately $30,000 per year how much they would need to make a year to consider themselves wealthy. Their average answer was around $74,000. When pollsters asked the same question to people who made approximately $50,000 a year, the average response was around $100,000 a year. Six-figure income earners answered that earning at least $500,000 would make them feel rich. And nearly everyone has heard the answer John D. Rockefeller, the world's first billionaire, gave to a similar question. When a reporter back in the early 1900s asked Rockefeller how much money was enough, the billionaire's classic answer was, "Just a little bit more."

The truth is that no matter how much we have, we think that just a little more will make us happy, but if I had two one-dollar bills and I threw them on the ground, very few people would get into a knock-down-drag-out fight to get them, would they? Yet more than three billion people—a little under half of the world's population—live on less than $2 a day. As of this writing, if you earn more than $45,000 a year, ranked by wealth, you're in the top one percent of people in the entire world.

So, if we're rich in comparison to more than half of the world, why are we running in a rat race to acquire more? It's because we don't have the right perspective.

A STEWARDSHIP PERSPECTIVE

In the last chapter, we looked at how God wants us to put our faith in Him as our source for everything in life, including our money and our possessions.

Let's revisit what Jesus said.

> For where your treasure is, there your heart will be also.

Matthew 6:21 NIV

Where your treasure is—how you're stewarding what God is giving you—is a reflection of what your heart is attached to. If you want to develop a heart for God's kingdom, put your treasure there. If you want to change your heart, change where you put your money.

That Scripture speaks volumes, but let's take it one step further.

> Above all else, guard your heart. For everything you do flows from it.
>
> Proverbs 4:23 NIV

In examining these two scriptures about the heart together, we see that your heart will be attached to the place where you put your treasure... and you need to guard that place above all else because everything you do and everything you have flows into your life through your heart. That's a sobering thought. It requires that we have the right perspective of our treasure (our finances, resources, and possessions) to be able to make sure that the things which flow into our lives are connected to a pure source in our hearts.

I believe that to understand and to live as one of God's faithful stewards is the most liberating lifestyle there is. The Bible has a lot to say about understanding stewardship, but we need to start by changing our perspective of possessions.

> The earth is the Lord's, and all its fullness, The world and those who dwell therein.
>
> Psalm 24:1 NKJV

Your perspective forms your concept of reality. Everything in the Earth—all of its fullness and everyone who lives here—belongs to God. God is the owner of everything, and we're called to steward what He entrusts to us. Some of us really love our stuff, but that's a problem because it's not really ours. It's God's. We're just called to manage it. From time to time, even those of us who know that God owns everything sometimes act as though He doesn't. (Nobody is perfect in this.)

THREE STEWARDSHIP PRINCIPLES

If God really does own everything, then it stands to reason that God has the right to do whatever He wants with it whenever He wants. As we begin to change our perspective, it's important to be guided by these three biblical principles in the area of stewardship.

1. **Every spending decision is a spiritual decision.**

    This may seem overly religious, but every spending decision you make really is a spiritual decision, no matter how small it is. If God owns everything, and we're just managers of what He gives us, then every time we make a purchase, we're making a spiritual decision. We're deciding on God's behalf where His kingdom resources should be spent. Many of us aren't experiencing God's blessing in our lives because we aren't completely surrendering His money and His possessions to Him. We should be asking, "God, what do you want me to do with what you've given me to manage?"

2. **God wants us to invest wisely and generously.**

    God wants us to invest the resources He has entrusted to us in things that matter and will produce a good return for His kingdom. God allows us to steward His resources for a purpose.

    A wise steward manages his master's resources with the goal of his owner in mind. As stewards in the kingdom of God, we are called to manage the finances God has given us with His goals in mind. We need to be kingdom minded and invest our resources in things that are eternal, not in a bunch of earthly treasures that won't last.

    A good steward protects and grows the owner's assets with fierce intensity because he understands the owner's goals. We need to invest our time, our talent, and our treasure prioritizing the things God values. We need to be wise money managers so none of the precious resources that God has entrusted to us are wasted.

    God wants us to invest in lasting treasure. He wants us to reach the world with the Gospel of Jesus Christ. It has been said that the story of your bank statement is the story of your life. It tells you what you believe. It tells you who and what you really care about. Does your bank statement match God's priorities for His kingdom?

God isn't looking for the person who can earn the most money, He's looking for a heart that asks, "How can I properly discern what God wants me to do with what He's entrusted to me?" The more wisdom you have about what God wants, the more resources you can be trusted with, and the more you will be given to manage.

> Wisdom is a shelter as money is a shelter, but the advantage of knowledge is this: Wisdom preserves those who have it.

Ecclesiastes 7:12 NIV

We don't necessarily need more money, but we do need to become better stewards of what we already have.

3. As stewards, God holds us accountable.

One day, we're going to find ourselves standing before God, and He's going to ask, "What did you do with what I gave you?" He's going to expect a response. He won't just be asking us what we did with our *money*. He'll be asking us, "What did you do with the *life* I gave you? What did you do with the *breath* I gave you? What did you do with the *relationships* I gave you?"

To hear Him say, "Well done, good and faithful servant," we must understand that God doesn't just reward faithfulness, but He also rewards our *fruitfulness*. There's a difference. You can be faithful at doing all the wrong things and living the wrong way. The servant who was only given one talent in Matthew 25 was *faithful,* but he wasn't *fruitful.* He buried his master's money and guarded it, but that was not what his master wanted. God wants us to be faithful at being fruitful.

God is going to take inventory of all the resources and relationships we had and of all our financial decisions. It's important that we not take lightly anything God has entrusted to us. Whether it's wisdom, influence, relationships, children, family members, time, finances, or some other resource, we have to recognize those things as gifts from Him. We need to be careful to embrace the responsibility that comes with the blessings God has given us. We have to be good stewards, knowing we will be held accountable for them when we meet Him face to face.

A WISE PLAN

The United States is supposed to be one of the richest nations on the planet, but I've never seen more doubt, fear, and insecurity around the subject of finances than I see in our society today. That's because our thoughts lead to habits. Our habits lead to our lifestyles, and our lifestyles lead to our destiny. It's not enough to have a little bit of skill and a good work ethic to keep your head above water when it comes to finances in our world. No, our thought patterns, habits, and lifestyles will either lead us to a place of financial freedom, peace, and confidence or to a cycle of debt, fear, and insecurity.

The debt epidemic in our nation seems to be at record levels, and it doesn't seem to be going away any time soon. But living in the cycle of debt isn't God's plan for His children.

God wants us to be WISER than the world.

> Behold, I send you out as sheep in the midst of wolves. Therefore be wise as serpents and harmless as doves.
>
> Matthew 10:16 NKJV

As believers, we're not supposed to use the dog-eat-dog tactics of the world's financial playbook, but we are supposed to be as wise as the world's best managers—and even **WISER**—when it comes to how this planet's resources flow through our hands. God's economy is higher and better than anything the world could ever give us.

As people who put our trust in the All-Sufficient God of the Universe, we shouldn't be held captive to the earthly cycles of debt that plague this world's population. But that doesn't mean God will rain money down on us from the sky. We have to work and develop skills to get it.

THE DANGER OF DEBT

Before you get upset, I do want to make one point clear. I'm *NOT* saying that if you're in debt, there's something wrong with you, or you're less of a Christian somehow. I'm also *NOT* saying that all debt is evil. I believe you should be wise about any debt, but I don't believe it's a sin to have any kind of debt. For example, Kyla and I have a house with a mortgage loan on it. Our interest rate is extremely low, and we're paying off our principal balance quickly. I don't believe God is upset about us having a loan which is tied to an asset, which hopefully will be appreciating over time. And as we have the finances in our budget to pay the mortgage off, Kyla and I will be systematically paying off the principal early.

However, if you're thinking of telling your spouse, *"Honey, this pastor from Texas just said in his book that it's okay for us to take out that loan to buy that expensive new, luxury car we can't afford,"* I'm afraid you've misunderstood me. A car is not an appreciating asset. The moment you drive it off the sales lot, it's worth less than when you got it. But maybe you're a business owner and you're saying, "Hey, we've had to leverage some debt to grow our business." That's not necessarily unwise if most of it is tied to your profits and future expansion. Again, I'm not saying debt is a sin. I'm saying that we just need to be wise when it comes to leveraging any part of the future for something in the here and now (and especially for something in the past).

God is calling His children to be wise. We have to look beyond the monthly payments and the annual interest rates. We have to look at the value of things over time versus the opportunity cost of what the total financed price will end up costing us in the future. We need to take a hard look at everything we spend our money on and everything we want to buy.

"Honey, can we really afford the house that we live in?" All your money might be going into a house you can't even afford. Many couples get starry-eyed when they get married.

Kyla and I made that mistake on our first house. We went into the worst neighborhood where we thought we could actually afford to buy a house. It was a fixer upper, and we had been watching HGTV every day. We went in thinking we were Chip and Joanna Gaines. We had a vision. We could see the "potential." Before that we wouldn't have even gone grocery shopping in that neighborhood! But we were determined we were going to buy a house and remodel it. The problem was that we didn't have the skills, the time, or the money to do it! We thought we could get to the same success level overnight that our parents took thirty years to achieve. Nope, it doesn't work that way. Fortunately we got out of that house when we moved to a new city, and we learned to change our cycle of bad debt. How did we change it? We changed what we believed.

IT'S TIME TO WAKE UP

> And do this, knowing the time, that now it is high time to awake out of sleep; for now our salvation is nearer than when we first believed.
>
> Romans 13:11 NKJV

It's time for us to wake up. It's time to stop being complacent and assuming that your circumstances always have to be the way they've been. The word translated as "salvation" in this verse is the Greek word "soteria," and it doesn't only mean *salvation* in a spiritual sense. It means *deliverance, protection, soundness, prosperity, health, and preservation.* This verse is saying the time for your freedom is now. The time for your freedom from sin is now. The time for your freedom from sickness and disease is now. And the time for your financial freedom is now.

Today, if you're fed up with debt collectors, juggling your bills, and living paycheck to paycheck, it's time to make a change. God wants more for you than barely getting by. God wants you to be blessed so that you can be a blessing and help establish His kingdom on the Earth.

> And you shall remember the Lord your God, for it is He who gives you power to get wealth, that He may establish His covenant which He swore to your fathers, as it is this day.

> Deuteronomy 8:18 NKJV

When I was in Israel, I went to see a giant body of water called the Dead Sea. Do you know why the Dead Sea is "dead"? It's because it has a lot of salt. Very few organisms can survive in its salty concoction. Salt and minerals in that water have accumulated over time because the "sea" isn't really a sea at all. It's a lake with inlets—but it has no outlets. Water flows in and it stays there. The water is "dead" because nothing ever flows out of it.

Some people are like the Dead Sea. Resources flow into their lives, but they never flow out. They're some of the meanest, angriest, and most stingy people you've ever met. Everything is coming in, but nothing is flowing out. They're unhappy because God created us to be conduits to help and to bless others with our lives. God wants us to be conduits or pipes that He can use to distribute blessings to others, and if you think about it, when the water is flowing to its intended destination, the pipes that deliver it get wet too.

In the same way that our God is generous, we, as His image bearers, should be generous too. I want to be able to say "yes" every time I see someone in need. I want to be able to have enough to take care of my family and plenty left over to be able to help people who are in need. But the reality is we can't say "yes" until we have said "no" to living beyond our means. We have to be able to stop debt from holding back our generosity. If we're living paycheck to paycheck, how much of a blessing can we really be?

Consumer debt is out of control in our world. Debt has literally shut down governments (Greece, Italy, Los Angeles, and Chicago in the last few years). The good ol' USA has an astronomical amount of debt (more than $20 *TRILLION* as of this writing), and if something doesn't change, even our great-great-great grandchildren will never be able to pay it off.

> Just as the rich rule the poor, so the borrower is servant to the lender.

> Proverbs 22:7 NLT

Debt strangles us. It mortgages our futures. It limits us and restricts our options in life. Debt obligates us to pay off yesterday's expenses with tomorrow's income.

Again, I don't think it's necessarily a sin to be in debt, but there are two types of people mentioned in the book of Proverbs. One is wise and one is foolish. There are wise Christians, and there are foolish Christians. We're all going to Heaven, but some of us are going to have a harder life between now and then because we've been unwise with our finances.

Debt doesn't just impact our bank accounts. It impacts us mentally, spiritually, emotionally, and relationally. Financial stress is cited as the number-one reason for divorce in our nation, and research has shown that people who struggle under the burden of crushing, long-term debt have more physical ailments which can be directly linked to the mental stress their financial situation has caused. Debt isn't simply a natural thing. There are actually spiritual forces behind it. Satan doesn't want God's children to be blessed because, when they are, they generously support the advancement of God's kingdom.

The good news is that God wants us to be stable and strong, living in healthy, positive, blessed environments of fulfillment, freedom, and enjoyment.

THE WAR ON DEBT

Here are some practical steps to help you attack your debt and to help you keep clear of it in the future.

1.   Realize that debt is your enemy.

The banker might be friendly, but he isn't your friend.

2. **Develop a vision for becoming debt free.**

Can you see yourself at some point in the future becoming debt free? Do you have a vision for a time when you won't have a car payment? Do you have a vision for a time when your credit card will be paid off? What does that look like? Imagine how you will feel. Instead of resigning yourself to the lie that you will always be in debt, create a better picture in your mind's eye of the day when you will be financially free. You need to have a vision for that.

3. **Find out how much debt you have.**

It amazes me how a lot of people who are struggling with debt don't even know how much they owe. When you ask them what they owe and what they need to live each month, they don't have a clue. You can't get to any destination if you don't know where you're starting from.

4. **Make a financial plan.**

You need to have a budget. (Does anybody know what that is anymore?) A wise steward should know where every penny goes. He pays attention to the details and makes sure that he's honoring the master's desires. I would suggest you focus on percentage budgeting, for example:

> ›   Return the tithe to God's house (10% of gross income)

> ›   Save for the future (10% of gross income)

> ›   Live on the rest (80% of gross income)

5. **Destroy your credit cards.**

Stop believing the lies that you deserve everything now. Don't be caught in the trap of zero interest for the first twelve months! Seventy percent of people who sign up for a "no-interest," introductory credit card end up paying all the interest and more because they don't pay off their balances in time. Do you think the credit card companies don't know that? They're betting against you! (The house always wins.)

6. **Learn to do without.**

   If you don't have the money to pay for it, don't buy it. Period. Delayed gratification will change your life.

7. **Pay cash.**

   I know it's crazy. I know it's complicated to get out of your car, and go in and give the gas station clerk $20 cash, when your tank could take $22.36, but pay cash for everything you possibly can. Statistics have actually shown that people spend up to thirty percent less when they have to pay cash than they do when they pay with plastic. Stop hating on the Benjamins!

8. **Pause before you purchase.**

   Don't make quick financial decisions, especially when it comes to major purchases. If you didn't check the prices and take your time, I don't care what kind of a deal you think you got, you didn't. You will not die without a new T.V. or a new sofa. You will not die without a car. I've heard people say things like, "But my transmission went out. I just need to go get a new car." A transmission is about $2,500. A new car is $25,000. (I'm sorry, but that doesn't make any sense!) Take time. Pause, and think about it.

By the way, these are all mistakes that I've made. My past relationship with debt isn't squeaky clean. I've made every single one of these mistakes and some of them more than once! I learned every one of these things the hard way. Hopefully, you won't have to do the same.

Thank God that no matter where we are financially today, we can all learn to become better stewards of the resources we have been given. As we seek to use them wisely and work to conquer debt's hold on us once and for all, we need to remember these key thoughts.

» Every spending decision is a spiritual decision.

» God wants us to invest wisely and generously.

» As stewards, God holds us accountable.

» Realize that debt is your enemy.

» Develop a vision for becoming debt free.

» Find out how much debt you have.

» Make a financial plan.

» Destroy your credit cards.

» Learn to do without.

» Pay cash.

» Pause before you purchase.

KEY THOUGHTS

» Every spending decision is a spiritual decision.
» God wants us to invest wisely and generously.
» As stewards, God holds us accountable.
» Realize that debt is your enemy.
» Develop a vision for becoming debt free.
» Find out how much debt you have.
» Make a financial plan.
» Destroy your credit cards.
» Learn to do without.
» Pay cash.
» Pause before you purchase.

CHAPTER 5

A WISE PLAN

SMALL GROUP AND DEVOTIONAL LESSONS

READ

As believers, we're not supposed to use the dog-eat-dog tactics of the world's financial playbook, but we are supposed to be as wise as the world's best managers—and even **WISER**—when it comes to how we steward or manage what God's put into our hands. **God wants us to be WISER than the world.**

God is calling His children to be wise with our wallets. We have to look beyond the monthly payments and the annual interest rates. We have to look at the value of things over time and the future opportunity cost versus the pleasure of the moment. **We need a wise plan**—a plan that's flexible over time and built on the principles found in the Bible. We need to learn how to budget wisely. **Every spending decision we make, no matter how small, is a spiritual decision.**

Debt is our enemy. It strangles us and mortgages our future. It limits us and restricts our options in life. Debt obligates us to pay off yesterday's expenses with tomorrow's income. Debt isn't just a natural thing; there are actually spiritual forces behind it. Our enemy, the devil, wants us to live in bondage to debt and unable to answer God's call to generosity. **As we apply practical wisdom, develop and live on a budget, and learn to handle debt wisely, we will experience greater freedom to act in God's economy.**

- -

☐ **DAY 1**   **Proverbs 29 and 1 Samuel 29**

☐ **DAY 2**   **Proverbs 30 and 1 Samuel 30**

☐ **DAY 3**   **Proverbs 31 and 1 Samuel 31**

☐ **DAY 4**   **1 Timothy 1 and 2 Samuel 1**

☐ **DAY 5**   **1 Timothy 2 and 2 Samuel 2**

☐ **DAY 6**   **1 Timothy 3 and 2 Samuel 3**

☐ **DAY 7**   **1 Timothy 4 and 2 Samuel 4**

◌◌◌◌◌ REFLECT ◌◌◌◌◌

1. How have you viewed budgeting and debt in the past, and how have these views positively or negatively impacted your life?

2. Discuss the natural strategies for fighting debt. Which one or two could you implement that would make the greatest impact in your situation?

◌◌◌◌◌ WRITE ◌◌◌◌◌

Journal your thoughts from the discussion questions here.

CHAPTER NOTES

A DILIGENT LIFE

A diligent life doesn't happen overnight. Everyone wants the pot of gold at the end of the rainbow, but few people are diligent enough to do what it takes to grow personally to achieve lasting success. Discipline, diligence, personal growth—call it what you will, but without it, you will never realize your full potential or receive all the blessings that God has in store for you.

> Don't you realize that in a race everyone runs, but only one person gets the prize? So run to win! All athletes are disciplined in their training. They do it to win a prize that will fade away, but we do it for an eternal prize. So I run with purpose in every step. I am not just shadowboxing. I discipline my body like an athlete, training it to do what it should....
>
> 1 Corinthians 9:24–27 NLT

Diligence brings personal growth, and personal growth produces success.

Life isn't a sprint. It's a marathon. Growth and development require diligence, endurance, and consistency.

THE TRIANGLE OF SUCCESS

Did you know that a triangle is the strongest geometric shape? Because of a triangle's inherent structural characteristics, its ability to distribute force evenly to all three sides makes it more stable than a square or a circle. Each individual side corresponds and is proportionate to its opposite angle, and it rests upon the vertex of the other two sides. That may not seem exciting to you, and you probably didn't pick up this book to relive the horrors of middle school math, but please bear with me in my love of triangles.

But, first, let me make it clear that we are always "in process." None of us has it all together. As much as we'd like to think we are exactly what we pretend we are in our social media profiles, we're not really that perfect. If we're honest about it, we could all say, "I'm not where I want to be yet, but I'm not where I used to be either." God is working in each and every one of us to help us become the people He created us to be.

> For we are His workmanship [His own master work, a work of art], created in Christ Jesus [reborn from above—spiritually transformed, renewed, ready to be used] for good works, which God prepared [for us] beforehand [taking paths which He set], so that we would walk in them [living the good life which He prearranged and made ready for us].
>
> Ephesians 2:10 AMP

To become spiritually transformed works of art, living the good life God prearranged and made ready for us, we have to understand how we grow.

And that takes us back to the triangle!

There are three parts to our personal growth and success, and they rest upon and are connected to each other like the parts of a triangle. If you take one away, the whole becomes incomplete. The three parts of the triangle of success are: **character, calling, and competence.**

Let's look at each of these individually.

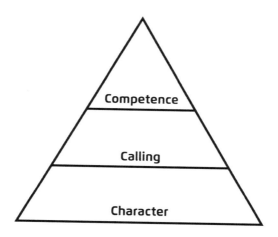

CHARACTER

The foundation of all personal growth and success is character. Character produces accountability.

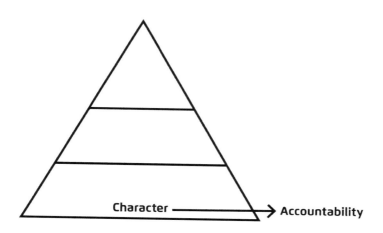

Character is defined as *the mental and moral qualities distinctive to an individual.* To see godly character in action, we need look no further than the life of Jesus.

After three days they found him in the temple courts, sitting among the teachers, listening to them and asking them questions. Everyone who heard him was amazed at his understanding and his answers. When his parents saw him, they were astonished.... "Why were you searching for me?" he asked. "Didn't you know I had to be in my Father's house?" ...Then he went down to Nazareth with them and was obedient to them.... And Jesus grew in wisdom and stature, and in favor with God and man.

Luke 2:46–52 NIV

Then Jesus was led by the Spirit into the wilderness to be tempted there by the devil. For forty days and forty nights he fasted and became very hungry. During that time the devil came and said to him, "If you are the Son of God, tell these stones to become loaves of bread." But Jesus told him, "No! The Scriptures say, 'People do not live by bread alone, but by every word that comes from the mouth of God.'" Then the devil took him to the holy city, Jerusalem, to the highest point of the Temple, and said, "If you are the Son of God, jump off! For the Scriptures say, 'He will order his angels to protect you. And they will hold you up with their hands so you won't even hurt your foot on a stone.'" Jesus responded, "The Scriptures also say, 'You must not test the Lord your God.'" Next the devil took him to the peak of a very high mountain and showed him all the kingdoms of the world and their glory. "I will give it all to you," he said, "if you will kneel down and worship me." "Get out of here, Satan," Jesus told him. "For the Scriptures say, 'You must worship the Lord your God and serve only him.'"

Matthew 4:1–10 NLT

We see four truths about developing godly character from the Bible passages found above.

1. **Character takes time to build.**

    Mary and Joseph could tell Jesus was a superstar when He was only twelve years old, but that wasn't when He started His ministry. For approximately eighteen years after this event, Jesus consistently obeyed and worked as a carpenter's apprentice, day after day after day. He was diligent in all His work, and God the Father was well pleased with Him. Even for Jesus, personal growth was a process.

2. **Character is built in obscurity.**

    Although some people believe Jesus did random miracles as a child, the Gospel of John tells us that isn't the case. Jesus developed His godly character over thirty years' time in relative obscurity. It wasn't until the wedding of Cana, where Jesus turned the water into wine, that He performed His first miracle (John 2:11). Even then, no one at the wedding, with the exception of Mary, the servants who filled the water pots, and possibly the host of the event, was aware of what Jesus had done.

3. **Character is proved when it is tested.**

    When Jesus was in the wilderness being tempted, He could have taken what seemed to be a shortcut to the position He knew was rightfully His. After forty days of fasting, Jesus certainly had a right to turn the nearest rock into a piping-hot loaf of bread. He had every right to command legions of angels to do His bidding if He should so desire, and He certainly knew that His rightful place of authority was to be lifted on high as King of kings and Lord of lords over all the kingdoms of the world—but it wasn't His time. Jesus wasn't willing to trade His character for a quick bagel and some instant gratification, no matter how much He may have wanted it at the time.

    There are three types of temptation Jesus faced, and every temptation you and I face will fall into these categories too.

> For everything in the world—the **lust of the flesh,** the **lust of the eyes,** and the **pride of life**—comes not from the Father but from the world.
>
>   1 John 2:16 NIV, Author's emphasis

> › **The lust of the flesh involves any type of sinful activity that will bring pleasure to the body.** These can include sexual sin, addictions, gluttony, uncontrolled anger or violence, and more.

> › **The lust of the eyes is a form of covetousness.** Although we rarely hear the term anymore, *to covet* means *to have a strong desire for something that rightfully belongs to another or for something which you haven't earned.* This is a big one when it comes to our finances. It's not just "those millennials" who often have a sense of entitlement. And let's not forget the overachievers who work at the expense of life, love, and home to gain status or recognition, or who are just consumed with the love of money, which is the root of all kinds of evil (1 Timothy 6:10 NIV).

> › **The pride of life is that desire for power that we all feel the temptation to attain.** Pride is one of the sins that God hates most. Some examples include the inordinate desire to make a name for ourselves, unteachableness, self-righteousness, an unwillingness to be accountable to anyone, and the desire to lord it over others.

We have to be careful not to let any kind of temptation destroy our character.

4.   Character is built on God's Word.

As Jesus responded to the enemy, He consistently spoke God's Word. But did you notice that the devil quoted God's Word too? What was the difference?

The difference was that Jesus not only spoke God's Word, He also *DID* it. Every day, day after day, Jesus obeyed God's Word.

CALLING

Character is the base of the triangle of personal growth and success, and **calling** is built upon its foundation. *Calling* is defined as *a strong urge toward a particular way of life or career; a vocation.* **Character produces accountability, and calling produces fruitfulness.**

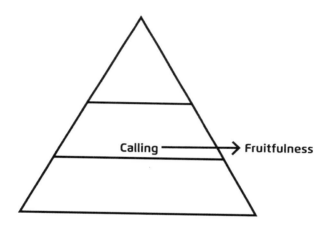

We're all building something, the questions we need to ask are: What are we building? How are we building it? And will it last? **Calling is about what we are building with our lives.**

God has called you to do more than just eat, sleep, and make money with the gifts He has given you. He wants you to build something eternal. God wants to increase your fruitfulness so that your life will have significance. You're called by God to get stuff done and to accomplish great things!

This is to my Father's glory, that you bear much fruit, showing yourselves to be my disciples.

John 15:8 NIV

Every believer is called to three things, and each of these callings produces fruit. Let's look at the Scriptures to learn what we're called to do.

» **We're called to follow Jesus.**

> Then He said to them, "Follow Me, and I will make you fishers of men"
>
> Matthew 4:19 NKJV

> But the Holy Spirit produces this kind of fruit in our lives: love, joy, peace, patience, kindness, goodness, faithfulness, gentleness, and self-control. There is no law against these things!
>
> Galatians 5:22–23 NLT

As we are connected to Jesus, the Holy Spirit produces fruit in our lives.

» **We're called to a local church family.**

The Church is a family.

> Do not rebuke an older man, but exhort him as a father, younger men as brothers, older women as mothers, younger women as sisters, with all purity.
>
> 1 Timothy 5:1–2 NKJV

And the Church is a body.

> All of you together are Christ's body, and each of you is a part of it.
>
> 1 Corinthians 12:27 NLT

You bear fruit in your local church when you are connected, growing, and leading. Staying committed to a church family helps you to realize you need them more than they need you. As you learn to navigate relationships there and grow, you can lead others and use your God-given gifts to help others grow too.

» **We're called to make a difference with our lives.**

> Work willingly at whatever you do, as though you were working for the Lord rather than for people. Remember

that the Lord will give you an inheritance as your reward, and that the Master you are serving is Christ.

Colossians 3:23–24 NLT

This third calling is unique to everyone. My wife is called to be a doctor. I am called to be a pastor. Everyone has special gifts and abilities that God has given them to use. These talents will help bring us finances to support His kingdom and our lives. We bear fruit in our callings (our vocations) as we succeed at reflecting Jesus in our spheres of influence.

The hand of the diligent will rule, But the lazy man will be put to forced labor.

Proverbs 12:24 NKJV

The more diligent we are in using our God-given gifts, the more successful we will be and the more lives we will reach.

COMPETENCE

The third part of the triangle of personal growth and success is **competence.** Competence is about *how* we do our work. The more competent we become—improving our natural skills and God-given talents—the more confident we will become. **Competence produces confidence.**

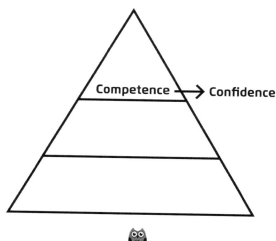

Competence is defined as *the combination of observable and measurable knowledge, skills, abilities and personal attributes that contribute to performance and success.*

Character produces accountability. Calling produces fruitfulness, and competence produces confidence.

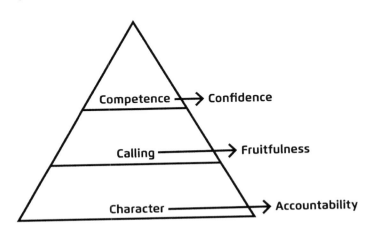

A lot of people can't wait until they turn sixty-five or seventy so they can quit their jobs, move to a house on the beach, and sip virgin piña coladas all day in retirement. That sounds nice. If you have enough money to quit working for a salary, you can quit your job. But as a believer in Christ Jesus, I have some news for you. You can't just unplug from the world and think you've finished all your work on this planet. Biblical retirement only happens when you die. If you're still breathing, God has big plans for you until you're not! He has problems for you to fix and people for you to reach for His kingdom.

THE PROBLEM WITH PROBLEMS

We tend to see problems as bad. If I'm honest, I struggle with this because I'm wired to walk into a room or an office and immediately see all the problems. Whether I'm standing in line at the check-out counter, waiting for the dentist, or standing in the auditorium of the church I pastor, my mind is always making mental notes of things that could be done better. The next day, if it's something under my power to take care of (and, admittedly, even when it's not) I usually just want to get after it and fix it.

The problem with problems is that we tend to look at them as if they're something negative. But in reality, problems are good. They give us a chance to innovate and create solutions. Problems provide opportunities for us to make something new and better out of the old. God uses us to make a difference by allowing us to fix the problems in our world. What if we saw opportunities when we looked at problems? What if we actually understood that our problems are simply stepping stones to something greater in our lives?

As Christians, we tend to think that Jesus came to solve all the world's problems, but that's not entirely true. He came to solve the world's biggest, deadliest problem—the sin problem—because it's the one we couldn't solve. With the help of the Holy Spirit, there are still some problems on this planet that Jesus expects us to solve. So, let's get to work!

SOME BIBLICAL IDEAS ABOUT WORK

Work is godly. Work is not a bad word. In the very first pages of Scripture we see God at work. The Earth was without form and void. In other words, there was a problem. God worked for six days, and the problem was solved.

Think of work as a chain reaction: the better you work—that is, the more competent you are at solving problems for other people—the more successful you will become. And the more successful you become, the more your financial resources will grow. It's that simple. This might sound harsh but as members of God's family, we love you no matter what, but as staff members of a company, you get paid to solve problems.

It's the spiritual law of *fair exchange*. As you benefit your employer in solving the company's problems with the God-given gifts you have and the knowledge you've acquired through instruction and experience, the company will bless you in return. And even if you work for the worst boss in the universe, if you work diligently as if you were working directly for the Lord, God will see to it that you are blessed (Colossians 3:22–24).

Here are four biblical principles about work that you need to understand if you're going to increase the level of your competence.

1. **We were created to work.**

    > The Lord God took the man and put him in the Garden of Eden to work it and take care of it.
    >
    > Genesis 2:15 NIV

    We are made in the image of God. He works, and so should we.

2. **Work can take us from a prison to a palace.**

    > So Pharaoh sent for Joseph, and he was quickly brought from the dungeon. When he had shaved and changed his clothes, he came before Pharaoh. Pharaoh said to Joseph, "I had a dream, and no one can interpret it. But I have heard it said of you that when you hear a dream you can interpret it."
    >
    > Genesis 41:14–15 NIV

    God used a problem to promote Joseph to the palace.

3. **Our work will continue in the new Heaven and new Earth.**

    Sorry, but we won't just be transformed into naked, baby angels floating on clouds.

    > Then God blessed them and said, "Be fruitful and multiply. Fill the earth and govern it. Reign over the fish in the sea, the birds in the sky, and all the animals that scurry along the ground."
    >
    > Genesis 1:28 NLT

    We're going to govern and take our places in leadership. The first man and woman were created to have dominion over

Creation before sin ever entered the picture, and Creation is going to go back to God's original plan.

4. **Our work prepares us to reign with Christ.**

> So I am willing to endure anything if it will bring salvation and eternal glory in Christ Jesus to those God has chosen. This is a trustworthy saying: If we die with him, we will also live with him. If we endure hardship, **we will reign with him.** If we deny him, he will deny us. If we are unfaithful, he remains faithful, for he cannot deny who he is.

> 2 Timothy 2:10–13 NLT, Author's emphasis

HEAD, HEART, AND HANDS

Diligence in our work qualifies us and makes us competent to lead, but not all leaders are qualified, and not all leaders are competent. Let's look at this in stories of two kings of Israel, Saul and David.

Up until the time of Saul, the nation of Israel had been governed by prophets, but the people decided they needed to have a king after they got tired of looking at the Facebook pages of all the neighboring countries (just kidding). The people decided they wanted to be like the nations around them and pleaded for a king, even though it wasn't best for them to be governed that way. You know the saying: *Be careful what you wish for....* God gave the people what they wanted in a king named Saul.

> Kish had a son named Saul, as handsome a young man as could be found anywhere in Israel, and he was a head taller than anyone else.

> 1 Samuel 9:2 NIV

Saul had natural talent. He was tall, smart, and good looking. He looked the part of a king. If he were alive today, Saul would easily have had more than a million Instagram followers. But Saul was a disaster spiritually.

David, on the other hand, didn't look like a king at all. He was a lowly, young shepherd boy. Even his own father didn't think David could lead.

> So he asked Jesse, "Are these all the sons you have?" "There is still the youngest," Jesse answered. "He is tending the sheep." Samuel said, "Send for him; we will not sit down until he arrives."
>
> 1 Samuel 16:11 NIV

Saul was discovered by people.

David was hidden by God.

Saul was what the people wanted.

David was what the people needed.

The overlooked shepherd boy, David, turned out to be the greatest leader of all the kings of Israel. He wasn't perfect. He made a lot of mistakes, but overall he was a godly leader. Why? Because he had the whole package: **head, hands, and heart.**

> But God removed Saul and replaced him with David, a man about whom God said, "I have found David son of Jesse, a man after my own heart. He will do everything I want him to do."
>
> Acts 13:22 NLT

> He [David] cared for them with a true heart and led them with skillful hands.
>
> Psalm 78:72 NLT

Because he had a true heart and he cared for his people, David was a great leader. He was a team builder. He rallied the troops of Israel after defeating Goliath (1 Samuel 17:50–53). He led a band of giant killers and mighty men (1 Samuel 23:8–39), and even when David faced a rebellion against his throne, the Scriptures say that everyone who was distressed, in debt, or discontented gathered themselves to David and followed him in the wilderness during his time of exile (1 Samuel 22:1–2).

You will soon discover, if you haven't already, that there will never be enough hours in a day or days in a week for you to get it all done. That's normal. God is expecting you to lead people skillfully and to help them grow along the way. Don't measure your competence by what you can do alone. God isn't calling you to be the best at everything. You just need to find out who is and give them the rails to run.

God isn't simply concerned about what we know, or even what we can do. He looks at the heart. He's looking for people who can lead with their heads, hands, and hearts. As we learn to develop our **character,** obey God in our **calling,** and build up our **competence,** it's important to remember these key points:

- » **Character takes time to build.**

- » **Character is built in obscurity.**

- » **Character is proved when it's tested.**

- » **Character is built on God's Word.**

- » **We're called to follow Jesus.**

- » **We're called to a local church family.**

- » **We're called to make a difference with our lives.**

- » **We were created to work.**

- » **Work can take us from a prison to a palace.**

- » **Our work will continue in the new Heaven and new Earth.**

- » **Our work prepares us to reign with Jesus.**

KEY THOUGHTS

» Character takes time to build.

» Character is built in obscurity.

» Character is proved when it's tested.

» Character is built on God's Word.

» We're called to follow Jesus.

» We're called to a local church family.

» We're called to make a difference with our lives.

» We were created to work.

» Work can take us from a prison to a palace.

» Our work will continue in the new Heaven and new Earth.

» Our work prepares us to reign with Jesus.

CHAPTER 6

A DILIGENT LIFE

SMALL GROUP AND
DEVOTIONAL LESSONS

⟳⟳⟳⟳⟳ READ ⟳⟳⟳⟳⟳

We've used the triangle to illustrate the strength of God's plan for building and stewarding wealth. Because of a triangle's even distribution of force to its three sides, it is more stable than other shapes. Like a triangle's parts, there are three parts to our personal growth that stabilize and make our lives stronger: **character, calling, and competence.**

The base of our lives and personal growth is character. Character takes the longest time to develop, but its foundation will determine how high and wide we can build. Although Jesus never sinned, He understands what we face, and He gave us the insight of His Word and the power of the Holy Spirit to grow in character and overcome temptation. We can know that our character is growing because growing **character always produces accountability.**

As our character develops, our calling is built upon its foundation. Our calling is that thing that we were put on Earth to do—to help make something better. What is our life's work? That's a big question, but an important one, as we talk about living a diligent life. **Calling always produces fruitfulness.**

Probably the most powerful part of the diligent life is competency. Competency is all about getting better at what we do—learning and developing skills over time. Diligence in our work qualifies us and makes us competent to lead others. **Competency produces confidence.**

☐ **DAY 1**   **1 Timothy 5 and 2 Samuel 5**

☐ **DAY 2**   **1 Timothy 6 and 2 Samuel 6**

☐ **DAY 3**   **2 Timothy 1 and 2 Samuel 7**

☐ **DAY 4**   **2 Timothy 2 and 2 Samuel 8**

☐ **DAY 5**   **2 Timothy 3 and 2 Samuel 9**

☐ **DAY 6**   **2 Timothy 4 and 2 Samuel 10**

☐ **DAY 7**   **Ecclesiastes 1 and 2 Samuel 11**

○○○○○ REFLECT ○○○○○

1. Why is character the foundation of a diligent life?

2. In which area or areas do you need to grow the most: character, calling, or competency? How will you go about growing?

○○○○○ WRITE ○○○○○

Journal your thoughts from the discussion questions here.

_____

_____

_____

_____

_____

_____

_____

_____

_____

_____

_____

_____

_____

_____

_____

_____

CHAPTER NOTES

CHAPTER 7

HONOR FIRST

In the world today, we have so many options. What do we want to wear? Will we have chicken or beef for dinner? What color do we want to dye our hair? What preschool do we want to put our three-year-old in, and how much money will we save to put him through college? Every day we're faced with literally hundreds of decisions we can make about our lives. In the midst of so many choices, we often feel paralyzed. What if we make the wrong decision or we do something that can't be undone? Fear and anxiety can creep in and cause us to miss out on God's best, especially in the area of our finances.

One of the best pieces of advice I've ever received was from my pastor and mentor. He told me that in moments when I don't know what to do, I should go back to what I do know. We'll hardly ever have all the answers or see the whole picture, but we can always go back to God's Word and apply the principles we are certain of.

We touched on the topic of honor in chapter three, but in this chapter, I want to explain more fully why honoring God with the tithe is so important for you to be able to walk in all the blessings God has for you in this life.

I have three kids whom I love dearly. I want what's best for them, and I want to do my very best to raise them in a way that allows them to succeed in God's plan for their lives. Sometimes this task seems overwhelming. I'll be honest. There have been times I've just wanted them to do what I say and trust me. When they were younger, all it took for them to be obedient was for me to tell them to do something, but, as they began to get older, they started to ask questions about what I asked them to do, and all their questions started with the word *why*.

Don't get me wrong. That's not a bad thing. God created us this way. We have a deep desire to understand the *why* behind the infinite *whats* of the world. As a father, I've come to realize that if I'm going to make a lasting impact in the lives of my children, I need to get comfortable with their questioning and the incessant *whys* after my every request. I am discovering that it's more important to teach my children *how to think* rather than simply *what to think*.

I've also come to see that, as I live out what I have learned about God from the Bible and simply model it for my kids, they are more likely to follow my example than my words. If I teach them how to think and show them how to act, they will always find their way back to God.

My goal in this chapter is to explain the *why* behind the *what* of tithing, in an effort that you would see the heart of God as the heart of a loving, Heavenly Father. Tithing isn't about rules and laws. It's about the Father's blessing for His children. When you understand the *why,* you can fully embrace the *what* of tithing and see the right choice in the midst of infinite options as it relates to this topic and to every other.

THE BEST MONEY ADVICE I EVER GOT

A member of our congregation asked me this question not too long ago: "Pastor, what's the best financial advice you ever received?"

I had to stop and think for a minute. I've had a lot of good financial mentors in my life through the years. These thoughts immediately started flooding into my mind.

» **Save Systematically.** I remember someone showed me a chart in one of Dave Ramsey's books, showing how two people who started saving money in retirement accounts, who both got the same rates of return, ended up at age sixty-five with their investments. The first person had started saving at age twenty by putting $2,000 a year into his account, and he continued this for ten years. The other guy started saving $2,000 each year at age thirty-five or forty, and he did this every year until he turned sixty-five, but he still hadn't caught up to the amount of money the person who started at age twenty had earned. The importance of educating myself on how the miracle of compound interest over time works was a very wise piece of financial advice I received.

» **Live Within Your Means.** I've had several mentors remind me of this important bit of financial wisdom: Don't buy stuff you don't need with money you don't have to impress people you don't even like. Keeping up with the Joneses might be okay for the Joneses, but for everyone else, it just leads to becoming broke.

» **Invest Wisely.** Diversify widely. Risk early while you can still recover. Keep things balanced, and then protect your nest egg at the end—all sound pieces of advice I've received from people through the years.

» **Marry Well.** If you bump into a guy or girl at college whose last name is Gates, Walton, or Buffett—give them a second look. Or just marry someone who is going to become a doctor, like I did. (Haha!)

That's all great advice, but it isn't the best advice you could ever get.

The best money advice you will ever get comes from a man who was the original financial genius. His name was Solomon. Back in the day, he topped the list of the world's wealthiest people. (Honestly, if you calculated out his wealth in today's dollars, he would still top the charts.) People talked about him all over the world. The book of Proverbs contains his wisdom about many areas of life, including finances. He was one of the first people to write down instructions about how to save systematically, live within your means, invest wisely, and marry well, and he also advised us to follow a financial principle that has the potential to revolutionize and transform not just your finances, but every area of your life. It's the **principle of the first.**

THE PRINCIPLE OF THE FIRST

> Honor the Lord with your possessions, And with the firstfruits of all your increase.
>
> Proverbs 3:9 NKJV

Solomon said that we were to honor the Lord with our firstfruits. It may seem simple, but let's start by looking at the definition of the word *first*. It means *to be the head of; the original; before all; in preference to something else; the foremost; the beginning.*

The principle of the first is very powerful. We find it throughout God's Word. God is Almighty. He is the Creator. Because He is the First, God desires to be first in our lives. We can give God the first of our time. We can give Him the first of our abilities. We can also give Him the first of our finances. He wants to be our first priority.

If we will put God first, we will be successful, and our needs will be met.

> But seek **first** the kingdom of God and His righteousness, and all these things shall be added to you.
>
> Matthew 6:33 NKJV, Author's emphasis

The way that we put God and His kingdom first is by making Him our first priority in every area of our lives, including the areas of our time, our talents, our families, our businesses, and our finances.

If you stop reading this book right here, I want you to take away this fact:

God must be first in everything.

If you do continue reading, I want to show you **three *firsts*** found in Scripture and the power of how they relate to our finances.

1. **The *first* must be dedicated to the Lord.**

> That you shall set apart to the Lord all that open the womb, that is, every firstborn that comes from an animal which you have; the males shall be the Lord's. But every firstborn of a donkey you shall redeem with the lamb....
>
> Exodus 13:12–13a NKJV

God says the firstborn belongs to Him. As this applied to animals in the Old Testament, the firstborn lamb from any ewe (or any animal that was considered to be "clean" in the Jewish Law) had to be sacrificed to the Lord. A firstborn donkey (or any animal that was considered "unclean") wasn't to be sacrificed. It had to be redeemed through the sacrifice of a lamb (or another "clean" animal) in its place.

I don't know about you, but I'm really glad that we don't live in that time in history any longer; however, the New Testament tells us that the things we find in the Old Testament are examples and symbols of things that are spiritual truths for us today (1 Corinthians 10:11). That means we need to look deeper into God's instruction in the Old Testament to find how it applies to us today.

Here's the spiritual principle behind the law of dedicating the firstborn to the Lord: Any creature that was deemed "unclean" according to God's Law had to be redeemed through the sacrifice of something "clean." You and I were born sinners, but the firstborn, spotless Lamb of God had to be sacrificed for our redemption. We were unclean. He was clean. There was nothing we could do to buy ourselves back from the kingdom of darkness. Only a pure and holy Lamb of God could pay the price for our salvation.

> But God demonstrates his own love for us in this: While we were still sinners, Christ died for us.
>
> Romans 5:8 NIV

While we were mocking Him and spitting on Him and nailing Him to the cross, He was dying for us. God didn't wait to see if we would change before He sacrificed His Son, Jesus. God gave us Jesus *first.* God gave Jesus in faith.

You could say it this way: **Jesus was God's tithe.** That's the way tithing is. Before you check to see whether you have enough, you give your tithe first in the same way that God gave Jesus first. Our money is redeemed, or blessed, as we give the first of our income to God. A lot of people talk about tithing, but they never understand *the principle of the first.* The *first* tenth of our income must be given to God in order to redeem the rest.

If you gave the firstborn lamb to God, you wouldn't know if your ewe was going to have any more lambs after that. God didn't say, "Wait until you have ten baby lambs, and then give Me one." This is what the firstborn and tithing is about. No, you had to sacrifice your *firstborn* lamb in faith. It's the same principle in giving the *first* ten percent of your income to God. Don't wait to make sure that all your other obligations are met before you return the first ten percent of your income to God.

Tithe *first.*

God says, "Give me the first, and the rest will be blessed." It's your faith that brings the blessing. The first belongs to God.

2. **The *firstfruits* must be brought into God's house.**

> The first of the firstfruits of your land you shall bring into the House of the Lord your God.
>
> Exodus 23:19a NKJV

Notice the Scripture designates "the House of the Lord" as the proper place to put our tithes, or firstfruits. Our tithes should be given to the local church where we worship. Some people wonder about tithing to a television ministry, a favorite missionary, or to a person in need. The Bible says we should give offerings to missions or charity works and give alms to the poor. But that's not the same as tithing. Giving to a missionary or other good work is something we do **AFTER** we pay our tithes. Tithes go directly to the local church.

Let's look at another place in the Bible that talks about *firstfruits.*

> Honor the Lord with your possessions, And with the firstfruits of all your increase.
>
> Proverbs 3:9 NKJV

This verse tells us not only to honor the Lord with our firstfruits (by bringing them to the Lord), but it also tells us what we are supposed to bring to Him. We are to bring Him the tithe (firstfruits) on **ALL our increase.** While most of us aren't farmers or making our living off of agriculture any more, it's clear that the tithe off any increase that we may receive belongs to God. That means our salaries, our bonuses, the profits from sales in our businesses, or the sale of property or homes we may own—whatever brings increase to us financially—the first ten percent of it belongs to God. If you purchased a house for $150,000, and sold it for $175,000, your increase was $25,000, and your tithe would be $2,500. If you make $30,000 a year in gross income, your tithe would be $3,000 to the local church where you worship.

Some people think that they can't afford to tithe off of all the increase the Lord gives them, but I'd like to challenge that thinking with a well-known story.

> *Years ago, a man came to Peter Marshall, the former chaplain of the United States Senate, with a concern about tithing. The man said, "I have a problem. I have been tithing for some time. It wasn't too difficult when I was making $20,000 a year. I could afford to give the $2,000. But now I am making $500,000 a year, and*

there is just no way I can afford to give away $50,000 a year."

Dr. Marshall reflected on the wealthy man's dilemma but gave no advice. He simply said, "Yes, I see that you have a problem. I think we should pray about it. Is that all right?"

The man agreed, so Dr. Marshall bowed his head and prayed, "Dear Lord, this man has a problem, and I pray that you will help him. Please reduce this man's salary back to the place where he can afford to tithe."

Nobody wants God to decrease their income so they're more comfortable with giving Him ten percent!

After Israel left Egypt and wandered in the wilderness, they finally came to the place when they would cross the Jordan River and follow Joshua into the Promised Land. It was there, in Jericho, that the Lord demonstrated that the firstfruits (the tithe) belong to Him.

> And the Lord said to Joshua: "See! I have given Jericho into your hand, its king, and the mighty men of valor." ...And the seventh time it happened, when the priests blew the trumpets, that Joshua said to the people: "Shout, for the Lord has given you the city! ...But all the silver and gold, and vessels of bronze and iron, are consecrated to the Lord; they shall come into the treasury of the Lord."
>
> Joshua 6:2, 16, 19 NKJV

The Israelites marched around Jericho seven times. They shouted. They blew trumpets, and the walls fell down, yet God told them that the spoils from the city belonged to Him. All of it was to be given to the Tabernacle.

At first glance, we might think: *That's not fair! Why does God want **ALL** of it? Shouldn't He only get ten percent?*

But God is righteous and just. He's the God who blesses us and not the god who takes away our blessings. The reason God wanted all the spoils from Jericho was because Jericho was the *first*. It was the first city in the Promised Land. God didn't ask the Israelites to give Him the spoils from any other city they conquered. He just asked for the first.

3. **If you'll give God the *first*, He'll bless the rest.**

This is still true today.

It was too bad that Achan didn't have faith that God would bless him with more. He entered Jericho and thought, *This might be the only city we conquer. I'm going to keep a little bit of the spoils.* (You can read about his disobedience in Joshua 6.)

First God called the gold and silver **consecrated** (Joshua 6:19), but after Achan took some of it for himself, one chapter later God called that same gold and silver **cursed** (Joshua 7:13).

As I mentioned earlier in this book, it's not God who curses people. That's not what God does or who He is. God was only pointing out the obvious. The spoils Achan stole were under a curse because he was depending upon the world's system to satisfy his needs rather than putting His faith in God's blessings. The firstfruits (your tithes) are consecrated and holy when you return them to the Lord's house, but if you take them for yourself, they're cursed.

FAQS ABOUT TITHING

We've looked at a lot of principles concerning tithing from stories in the Bible, but I know there are people who are reading this book who still may not be sure if they can take the step and really practice it, so I want to answer a few frequently asked questions I get as a pastor regarding the subject of tithing. Hopefully, this will help those who have been struggling in the past to go ahead and take God up on His challenge.

> "Bring the whole tithe into the storehouse, that there may be food in my house. Test me in this," says the Lord Almighty, "and see if I will not throw open the floodgates of heaven and pour out so much blessing that there will not be room enough to store it. I will prevent pests from devouring your crops, and the vines in your fields will not drop their fruit before it is ripe," says the Lord Almighty. "Then all the nations will call you blessed, for yours will be a delightful land," says the Lord Almighty.
>
> Malachi 3:10–12 NIV

Q: Isn't tithing under the Law?

A: Tithing was instituted before the Law and continues on after it.

Have you ever thought about why God accepted Abel's sacrifice but not Cain's offering?

> And in the process of time, it came to pass that Cain brought an offering of the fruit of the ground to the Lord. Abel also brought of the firstborn of his flock and of their fat, and the Lord respected Abel and his offering, but he did not respect Cain and his offering....
>
> Genesis 4:3–5a NKJV

"And in the process of time..." That's a very important phrase. Abel raised livestock, and Cain tilled the ground, but only Abel returned the first of his increase to God. Cain waited to make sure he had enough, and then he gave. He didn't bring the firstfruits. And God said, "I'm not accepting that."

The principle of the tithe, bringing the first of your increase to the Lord, came before the Law, way back in the Garden of Eden. It continued through the time of the Law, and into the New Testament and beyond into the Church, where Jesus affirmed tithing during His ministry on Earth

(Matthew 23:23), and today, where He Himself receives our tithes as our High Priest in the throne room of Heaven (Hebrews 7:8).

Q: When should we tithe?

A: We should tithe as soon as we get paid.

> And all the tithe of the land, whether of the seed of the land or of the fruit of the tree, is the Lord's. It is holy to the Lord.
>
> Leviticus 27:30 NKJV

Every time I get paid and pay my tithe, it reminds me that God comes first. Tithing first cuts the strings between my heart and my treasure. It reminds me that materialism is a losing battle, that more isn't better, that money isn't the answer, and that what I have isn't my own. It reminds me that God owns it all, and that, one day, I will give an account of what I did with God's stuff.

Every time we get paid, we have an opportunity to pass God's test. Actions speak louder than words. What are our actions saying to God? Do we really honor God above anything else? We can say that God is first in our lives, but we can look in our wallets and actually see who is first. We might find out it's really the mortgage company, the electric company, Target, or Academy Sports.

Q: Why is the tithe ten percent?

A: The Hebrew word for _tithe_ means _tenth part._

The Hebrew word for _tithe is_ "maa'ser," meaning _tenth part._ It comes from the root word "a'sar," meaning _tenth._

> And this stone, which I have set up for a pillar, shall be God's house. And of all that you give me I will give a full tenth to you.
>
> Genesis 28:22 ESV

Tithing teaches us that faith and honoring God makes the ninety percent with His blessing go further than one hundred percent without His blessing. As you tithe, your finances are redeemed from this cursed world we live in.

Giving God ten percent doesn't make sense in the world's system, but I'm telling you, from a biblical perspective and from my own personal life experience, it just works out.

Q: Is tithing just a payment plan to buy God's blessings?

A: Tithing isn't just a robotic thing we do. It's a matter of the heart.

> Honor the Lord with your possessions, And with the firstfruits of all your increase; So your barns will be filled with plenty, And your vats will overflow with new wine.
>
> Proverbs 3:9–10 NKJV

When we put God first in our hearts and our wallets, it opens His windows of blessing to us (Malachi 3:10). God's heart is to bless His children with every good thing that they need, spiritually, mentally, physically, and financially (2 Peter 1:3). He is our loving Heavenly Father, and it pleases Him to bless us (Luke 12:32). And as we turn our hearts toward Him and honor Him first with the tithe of our increase, we can believe that His promises will come to pass in our lives.

Let's remember these key thoughts as we return our tithes to the Lord:

» **God must be first in everything.**

» **The *first* is to be dedicated to the Lord.**

» **The *firstfruits* must be brought into God's house.**

» **If you'll give God the *first*, He'll bless the rest.**

» **Tithing was instituted before the Law and continues on after it.**

» We should tithe as soon as we get paid.

» The Hebrew word for *tithe* means *tenth part.*

» Tithing isn't just a robotic thing we do. It's a matter of the heart.

KEY THOUGHTS

» God must be first in everything.

» The *first* is to be dedicated to the Lord.

» The *firstfruits* must be brought into God's house.

» If you'll give God the *first*, He'll bless the rest.

» Tithing was instituted before the Law and continues on after it.

» We should tithe as soon as we get paid.

» The Hebrew word for *tithe* means *tenth part.*

» Tithing isn't just a robotic thing we do. It's a matter of the heart.

CHAPTER 7

HONOR FIRST

SMALL GROUP AND DEVOTIONAL LESSONS

⚬⚬⚬⚬⚬ READ ⚬⚬⚬⚬⚬

The best money advice we will ever receive comes from one of the wisest men who ever lived, Solomon. In Proverbs 3:9, he introduces us to **the principle of the first.** Solomon admonishes us to honor God with our possessions and with the first of ALL of our increase. We find this powerful principle throughout God's Word. If we put God first, He will meet all of our needs, and we will be successful.

God is so generous. He never tells us to do something that won't bless us. Malachi 3 says that the purpose of putting God first in our finances and returning the tithe (ten percent of our increase) to Him is to redeem our finances from the world's system. In the world's system resources are cursed. (Just read the first five chapters of Genesis to see that.) When we honor God with the tithe, He rebukes the devourer from the rest of our finances. **If we'll give God the *first,* He'll bless the rest.**

How does this work in our lives practically? Every time we get paid, *before* we pay anything else, we take the first ten percent and return it to God's house, the local church. The tithe is first. It is to be returned to God in faith, believing that He will bless the rest. By honoring God with the first, we're putting our trust and peace completely in Him to meet our needs. Trusting in Him is the only true security in life. **Tithing is a matter of the heart.**

- -

☐ **DAY 1**   **Ecclesiastes 2 and 2 Samuel 12**

☐ **DAY 2**   **Ecclesiastes 3 and 2 Samuel 13**

☐ **DAY 3**   **Ecclesiastes 4 and 2 Samuel 14**

☐ **DAY 4**   **Ecclesiastes 5 and 2 Samuel 15**

☐ **DAY 5**   **Ecclesiastes 6 and 2 Samuel 16**

☐ **DAY 6**   **Ecclesiastes 7 and 2 Samuel 17**

☐ **DAY 7**   **Ecclesiastes 8 and 2 Samuel 18**

✪✪✪✪✪ REFLECT ✪✪✪✪✪

1. Do you believe in honoring God with the tithe? Why or why not?

2. How does returning the tithe differ from giving offerings or helping those in need? Do you think that one is more important than the other, and if so, why do you feel that way?

✪✪✪✪✪ WRITE ✪✪✪✪✪

Journal your thoughts from the discussion questions here.

_____

_____

_____

_____

_____

_____

_____

_____

_____

_____

_____

_____

_____

CHAPTER NOTES

GENEROUS FAITH

Now to Him who is able to do exceedingly abundantly above all that we ask or think, according to the power that works in us...

Ephesians 3:20 NKJV

God is a giving God. He gave us His Son, Jesus, and bought us back from a life of living in the kingdom of darkness. He paid the ultimate price for us and canceled the debt we could never pay. As we reflect upon all that Jesus has done for us, our natural response should be to surrender our lives and everything in them to Him. As we hear His voice and obey everything He is telling us to do, we can be confident to sit back and watch Him do exceedingly abundantly above anything that we could ever have thought or dreamed. And because God is abundantly generous, we can be generous as well. If we'll trust Him completely, God can take our generosity and multiply it beyond our wildest imagination.

NATURAL AND SUPERNATURAL BLESSINGS

We've covered both the principles and the practical applications of **wisdom, diligence,** and **honor** in previous chapters so that we can clearly see how to get resources for ourselves and for our families. Applying those three principles is the primary way that we can be blessed financially, but now we're going to wrap things up by looking at the supernatural blessings God has for us.

The word *supernatural* is a compound word that indicates there are two parts. There's a *natural* part. (That's our part.) And there's a part that's *super*—meaning a part that's "above the natural." (That's God's part.) We need to do our part and believe God to do His part. To provide for us, God will do amazing miracles that are exceedingly abundantly above what we could ever imagine, but He requires us to be involved in our own help.

If we want to be blessed over and above just our needs being met so that we can become a blessing to others and leave a legacy, then there are two things we need to do on our part. Once we've done these things, God will do His part—the supernatural part.

» **Be faithful where you are.**

Whoever can be faithful with very little can also be trusted with much, and whoever is dishonest with very little will also be dishonest with much.

Luke 16:10, Author's paraphrase

God holds us accountable for being faithful with what we have, not for what we don't have. **Being faithful with your resources means always paying your tithe first.**

Kyla and I got married in 2005. She turned eighteen in April of that year, and we got married in June. Right away, we moved to St. Louis to help plant a church. (If you're a teenager, don't do it that way, but that's the way we did it). We didn't have jobs yet, but we had $1,600 cash that we had received from people as wedding gifts. We found a little apartment that required a payment of the first and last months' rent totaling $1,200, so we would still have $400 cash if we decided to sign the lease.

Kyla and I both grew up in homes that taught the principle of tithing. It was really easy to tithe when we lived at home.

When all the financial problems are your parents' problems, it's not difficult to tithe. But things were different all of a sudden. Kyla and I were out on our own, and we hadn't tithed off of the $1,600 cash that we had received from our wedding.

And then this revelation hit us. If we paid our tithe of $160 plus the $1,200 for the apartment, we would only have $240 left to live on. We were living in a strange town all by ourselves, with no groceries, no jobs, and no family or friends nearby to help us out. I remember looking at my wife and saying, "This is hard." I didn't want to pay the tithe. I wanted to keep it.

But then Kyla looked at me and said, "Stephen, more than ever, we need that $240 to be as blessed as it can possibly be blessed, because it's going to be at least a month before we get jobs. We're going to trust God and tithe." And we did.

Somehow, through a series of miraculous events, nine or ten months later, we had already made more in that year than both of our parents' annual incomes combined. (God always comes through when you're faithful.)

If you're thinking, I can't afford to be faithful, I'm telling you, you can't afford *NOT* to be faithful. Jesus said if you're faithful, you can be trusted. As you're faithful, God will trust you with more.

I can't put it any plainer than this: Being faithful with your finances means always paying your tithe first.

» **Give generously.**

Now he who supplies seed to the sower and bread for food will also supply and increase your store of seed and will enlarge the harvest of your righteousness.

2 Corinthians 9:10 NIV

The blessings of this verse tell us that God gives us seed to sow and bread for food. Not only that, but He will also increase the seed (money to give) of the person who is generous—*BUT* we have to understand this important truth: **Generosity begins at eleven percent!**

Assuming that we are tithing the first ten percent to God, then why aren't more believers blessed over and above just what they need to get by? Why do many wonderful people who follow Jesus Christ live paycheck to paycheck and never see the supernatural blessings that God wants to give them? For many, it's because they don't ever sow (beyond the tithe). They don't give because they're scared. They're scared because they think they're owners. If you rent a house or an apartment, are you afraid when the water heater goes out? No, you just call up your landlord. He's the owner, so he has to take care of the problem.

Let me encourage you to step out and be generous. God owns everything in the universe and beyond. He's right there with you. He'll never leave you. He has your back. The sooner you begin to trust God's plan for you, the more you'll see of His provision in your life.

Don't wait until you're out of debt to begin to give generously. You need to put your seed into the ground in order to receive the harvest. When you give out of a grateful heart and honor God in the tithe, God promises that He will rebuke the devourer in your life. God will supernaturally move mountains of debt for you when you bless others and support His kingdom!

God is a debt-canceling God. Perhaps you remember the story about Elisha and the widow's oil. The widow's husband had died, and the debt collector was coming to take her two sons as slaves to work off her debts. The woman had nothing in the house of any value except a little jar of oil. Elisha told her to borrow as many empty bowls and jars as she could find and to shut the door behind her while she poured the oil into the empty containers. Then God took over and multiplied the oil until it filled every bowl, jar, and bottle she had. She did what she could do in the natural, and God did what only God could do in the supernatural. Not only was the widow able to sell the oil and pay off her debt, she had more than enough to live off of for years! (See 2 Kings 4:1–7.)

We don't have to live in fear or doubt. We can give generously because we serve a God who multiplies oil, raises the dead, feeds crowds of thousands, sees every sparrow that falls, and knows how many hairs are on our heads.

> Give, and it will be given to you. A good measure, pressed down, shaken together and running over, will be poured into your lap. For with the measure you use, it will be measured to you.
>
> Luke 6:38 NIV

When God tells us to give and promises that He will bless us in return, we can take Him at His Word.

God gives us the power and the provision to get out and stay out of debt. He wants us to be good stewards and to break the cycle of debt in our lives. God doesn't want us to barely get by. He has miraculous provision in store for us if we'll be faithful with our resources and give generously. Once we've done our part, God will multiply the seed we've sown, supply more for us to give, and enlarge the harvest of our righteousness.

Let's look at some familiar biblical examples of how God multiplied the gifts of His servants.

THE MAKING OF A MIRACLE

> Some time after this Jesus crossed to the far shore of the Sea of Galilee... and a great crowd of people followed him because they saw the signs he had performed by

healing the sick. Then Jesus went up on a mountainside and sat down with his disciples. ...When Jesus looked up and saw a great crowd coming toward him, he said to Philip, "Where shall we buy bread for these people to eat?" He asked this only to test him, for he already had in mind what he was going to do. Philip answered him, "It would take more than half a year's wages to buy enough bread for each one to have a bite!" ...Andrew, Simon Peter's brother, spoke up, "Here is a boy with five small barley loaves and two small fish, but how far will they go among so many?" Jesus said, "Have the people sit down." There was plenty of grass in that place, and they sat down (about five thousand men were there). Jesus then took the loaves, gave thanks, and distributed to those who were seated as much as they wanted. He did the same with the fish. When they had all had enough to eat, he said to his disciples, "Gather the pieces that are left over. Let nothing be wasted." So they gathered them and filled twelve baskets with the pieces of the five barley loaves left over by those who had eaten.

John 6:1–13 NIV

In this passage we can see three key ingredients for a biblical miracle of generosity.

1.   Generosity begins where there is a need.

At this point in history, the common people were never too far from starvation. The people in Jesus' time could not afford to miss a few meals the way many of us can today. Many of the people in Israel, being under the harsh occupation and heavy taxation of Rome, lived off of barely what they needed to survive.

Jesus had been teaching all day, and the crowd had traveled hours to see Him. He knew the people were hungry, and He knew His Father would use those circumstances as a platform to demonstrate His love and His glory.

How did this miracle begin? It wasn't with faith. It wasn't with prayer. **It started with a need.**

All throughout Scripture, every miracle began where there was a need or a problem. The good news for us is that we all have problems. That means that we're candidates for a miracle. If we have big problems, we are in the perfect position to receive big miracles. In fact, the only people who have a real problem are the people who don't have problems because that means they don't need God!

2. **Generosity begins where there is a need, sensed by a person or a group.**

When we look at the story recorded in the sixth chapter of Mark's Gospel of the feeding of the multitude, we learn that Philip was not the only one to understand the need. All of the disciples realized that there was a problem. It was at the end of the day, and they had a big, hungry crowd they needed to feed. I'm sure they were hearing some criticism from the people about Jesus and His team not being prepared.

What did the disciples do about the problem? They brought the need to Jesus. That was a smart thing to do. When we have problems, we can bring them to Jesus. Jesus is never caught off guard with the challenges we face. He wants to help us through them. Jesus has a solution for every problem we have, but His answers require our obedience.

What do many Christians do when they have a problem? They step back and cheer God on. They sing songs to Him and even quote Scriptures to Him, but they often struggle to get involved with His plan when they're in need. They want God to do miracles without their participation. They're not looking for God to do a miracle; they're looking for magic! But that's not how God works.

In this story, God involved a lot of people in His miracle.

But He answered, "You give them something to eat."

Mark 6:37a NIV

Jesus involved His disciples. We all know God can do great things without us—but, for whatever reason, in His infinite wisdom, He asks His people to be a part of His work.

› God wanted to protect Noah's family from destruction, so He told Noah to build an ark.

› God wanted to save the people of Israel from annihilation by the Egyptians, so He told Moses to stretch his staff out over the Red Sea.

› God wanted to save His people from idolatry, so He told Elijah to stage a standoff against the prophets of Baal.

› Jesus wanted to heal the paralyzed man at the community pool, so He told him to pick up his mat and walk.

God is a loving, generous, exceedingly-abundantly-above-all-we-could-ask-or-think God, but He wants us to be involved in our own miracles.

3. **Generosity begins where there is a need, sensed by a person or a group, who step out in faith in spite of their fear.**

"Here is a boy with five small barley loaves and two small fish, but how far will they go among so many?"

John 6:9 NIV

Try to picture this situation. The disciples were having a hard time. Jesus had asked them to find enough food for more than five thousand people—so there they were, walking through the crowd looking for someone with a lunch. And then they found Little Jimmy.

I imagine that Little Jimmy probably hid his lunch when the disciples first started walking toward him. That's only natural. When we have something we feel is precious or scarce, the way this little boy probably felt about his lunch, it's often hard to give it up.

> **Sometimes we're not willing to give our resources to Jesus because we're comfortable.**

There was only one person in the crowd who didn't think he needed a miracle from God. It was Jimmy! The kid had food. He was the only one who thought ahead. The challenge with getting too comfortable with all our stuff is that we don't realize God has helped us so that we can help others.

There's a name for that in the study of psychology. It's called the "Bystander Effect." The "Bystander Effect" is a psychological phenomenon that refers to cases where individuals fail to offer assistance to a victim in an emergency situation when other people are present. In fact, the probability of a person helping a victim is inversely proportional to the number of bystanders present on the scene. In other words, the greater the number of people around in an emergency, the *LESS* likely it is that any one of those people will help. Bystanders in a crowd see the need but assume that others will step in instead of taking on the responsibility themselves.

> **Another reason we often won't give up our resources to Jesus is because sometimes it seems that what He's asking us to do doesn't make sense.**

In the story with Little Jimmy, it was five thousand men and their families versus one lunch. (I'm from Texas, and that's like feeding a sell-out crowd at a Mavericks game with one McDonald's super value meal.) That doesn't work in the natural, but faith gives because God asks for it, not because it makes sense.

Maybe you feel as if all you have is a tiny amount of resources. But God isn't looking at the size of your lunch box or your wallet. He's looking at your faith and obedience.

Can you imagine Jimmy at the end of the day when he told everyone at home what had happened? **From that time on, his life was marked by the day he gave his lunch to Jesus.** I imagine he told the story a hundred times. At the family reunion, I'll bet his kids and grandkids would moan and say, "Oh, no! There he goes with the lunch story again!"

If Little Jimmy could step out today and say one thing to us, here's what he would probably say: **God multiplies whatever you offer Him.** In the hands of Little Jimmy, those loaves of bread and fish were only one meal, but in the hands of Jesus, they were a feast for a multitude.

As we listen to the voice of God, we'll hear the Lord saying, "Give me your lunch. Put it in my hands and trust Me. Let me do something miraculous with it."

GENEROSITY PURSUES THE VISION OF GOD

The little boy who gave His lunch to Jesus was willing to lay down the smallness of only feeding himself. He stepped out in faith to surrender his resources to God's larger purposes. God is challenging us to do the same. It's a wonder to me that many Christians will surrender their hearts to God, yet they can't seem to take the step to surrender their wallets to Him.

"For I know the plans I have for you," declares the Lord, "plans to prosper you and not to harm you, plans to give you hope and a future. Then you will call on me and come and pray to me, and I will listen to you."

Jeremiah 29:11–12 NIV

God can be trusted. His plans are much bigger, better, and **WISER** than we could ever think up in our wildest dreams.

> "For my thoughts are not your thoughts, neither are your ways my ways," declares the Lord. "As the heavens are higher than the earth, so are my ways higher than your ways and my thoughts than your thoughts."

> Isaiah 55:8–9 NIV

As we align ourselves with God's purposes, blessings will flow through and into our lives. We are the conduits that God wants to use to bring His blessings and glory into this broken world. Remember, when the water of blessing is flowing, the pipes are the first to get wet.

But don't misunderstand. Giving God our time, talent, and treasure isn't some cheap get-rich-quick scheme. No, generosity is a lifelong commitment to follow God's plan and to build His kingdom. God doesn't owe us anything, but we owe Him *EVERYTHING*.

People with a generous heart put the kingdom of God before their own needs and desires. They purposefully give to further the kingdom— and God doesn't let their giving go unnoticed.

> Let each one give [thoughtfully and with purpose] just as he has decided in his heart, not grudgingly or under compulsion, for God loves a cheerful giver [and delights in the one whose heart is in his gift].

> 2 Corinthians 9:7 AMP

I think this is best illustrated in the story found in the book of First Chronicles, when David wanted to build a Temple for the Lord. It was time for the children of Israel to move forward into the next step of God's vision for them. They needed to create a permanent place of worship for God. As David handed over the throne to his son Solomon, he charged the people of Israel in a project to create a place where the whole nation could worship God.

> ...King David said to all the assembly: "My son Solomon, whom alone God has chosen, is young and

inexperienced; and the work is great, because the temple is not for man but for the Lord God. Now for the house of my God I have prepared with all my might: gold... silver... bronze... iron... wood... onyx... all kinds of precious stones, and marble slabs in abundance. Moreover, because I have set my affection on the house of my God, I have given to the house of my God, over and above all that I have prepared for the holy house, my own special treasure of gold and silver: three thousand talents of gold... and seven thousand talents of refined silver, to overlay the walls of the houses; ...and for all kinds of work to be done by the hands of craftsmen. Who then is willing to consecrate himself this day to the Lord?" Then the leaders of the fathers' houses, leaders of the tribes of Israel, the captains of thousands and of hundreds, with the officers over the king's work, offered willingly. They gave for the work of the house of God five thousand talents and ten thousand darics of gold, ten thousand talents of silver, eighteen thousand talents of bronze, and one hundred thousand talents of iron. And whoever had precious stones gave them to the treasury of the house of the Lord.... Then the people rejoiced, for they had offered willingly, because with a loyal heart they had offered willingly to the Lord; and King David also rejoiced greatly.

1 Chronicles 29:1–9 NKJV

From this story, we can see five important truths about pursing God's vision with a generous heart.

1.   The generous realize God's vision is bigger than their own.

"...The work is great, because the temple is not for man but for the Lord God."

1 Chronicles 29:1 NKJV

One of David's greatest desires was to build a permanent dwelling place for the presence of God, but David knew it would be up to Solomon and the next generation to carry on this task. David knew the task was greater than one man could accomplish. It would take all the people contributing for the Temple to become what it was meant to be. As God's people, we must realize that it isn't just the job of the pastor or of the church staff to build the kingdom of God. Because the work is great and God's vision is big, the task belongs to all of us together.

2.   The generous set their affection on the house of God.

"...Because I have set my affection on the house of my God, I have given..."

1 Chronicles 29:3 NKJV

David set his heart, his affection, and his resources on the house of God. He knew it was his responsibility to lead the people in fulfilling God's vision. There are many places where we can invest our time, our talent, and our treasures. However, there is none more powerful than the local church.

The local church is the hope of the world. The Federal Government, the Red Cross, and the university systems are not meant to be the primary change agents of the world. Relief agencies were not commanded by Jesus to turn the world upside-down. The local church is commanded to go out, reach the world, care for the hurting, encourage the lonely, and set them in families. **It is the Church's responsibility to transform this world through the love of Jesus Christ.**

3.   The generous give over and above.

"...I have given to the house of my God, over and above all that I have prepared for the holy house, my own special treasure of gold and silver."

1 Chronicles 29:3 NKJV

David was a tither, and David also gave extravagant, over-and-above offerings to the Lord. Remember, God is looking for good stewards. The Bible says that he who sows generously will reap generously. God provides seed to the person who sows extravagantly into His kingdom. **God supernaturally multiplies your seed—the over-and-above offerings—that you give to Him.**

4. **True disciples offer their gifts generously, willingly, and first.**

    "...Who then is willing to consecrate himself this day to the Lord?" Then the leaders of the fathers' houses, leaders of the tribes of Israel, the captains of thousands and of hundreds, with the officers over the king's work, offered willingly.

    1 Chronicles 29:5–6 NKJV

In the Greek, the word *disciple* and the word *leader* are the same word. If we say we are disciples of Jesus, then we are called to be leaders for those around us. You may not think that you're a leader, but you are. A leader is simply someone who influences others for action. A true disciple, or leader, takes the first step and encourages others to follow. And a disciple doesn't separate his or her finances from their faith. This is a spiritual challenge that requires a natural response. I think it's interesting that David challenged the leaders to go first. **Leaders always set the stage. True disciples lead.**

5. **Generosity is contagious.**

    Then the people rejoiced, for they had offered willingly, because with a loyal heart they had offered willingly to the Lord...

    1 Chronicles 29:9 NKJV

After the leaders gave generously, all the people of Israel gave generously too. Giving generously to God's vision inspires others. **Generosity is contagious.** When God's people have a generous heart, it not only builds God's kingdom, but they also get blessed in their giving. Generosity brings joy to everyone involved. And best of all, generous giving brings God joy!

...God loves a cheerful giver.

2 Corinthians 9:7b NKJV

Generosity isn't about money. It's a spiritual force. God loves it when His children are generous with their resources because it demonstrates that we are His image bearers. Jesus said that the world would know we are His disciples because of our love. Love gives generously. And as we sow generously into building lives for God's glory, God will bring us a bountiful harvest so that we can give again.

As we close this chapter, let's remember these key points about being generous.

» **First, be faithful where you are.**

» **Give generously.**

» **Generosity begins where there is a need, sensed by a person or a group, who step out in faith in spite of their fear.**

» **The generous realize God's vision is bigger than their own.**

» **The generous set their affection on the house of God.**

» **The generous give over and above.**

» **True disciples offer their gifts generously, willingly, and first.**

» **Generosity is contagious.**

KEY THOUGHTS

» **First, be faithful where you are.**

» **Give generously.**

» **Generosity begins where there is a need, sensed by a person or a group, who step out in faith in spite of their fear.**

» **The generous realize God's vision is bigger than their own.**

» **The generous set their affection on the house of God.**

» **The generous give over and above.**

» **True disciples offer their gifts generously, willingly, and first.**

» **Generosity is contagious.**

CHAPTER 8

GENEROUS FAITH

SMALL GROUP AND
DEVOTIONAL LESSONS

⟲⟲⟲⟲⟲ READ ⟲⟲⟲⟲⟲

Applying the principles of wisdom, diligence, and honor is the primary way we can be blessed financially, but there's another application to the principle of faith that releases the supernatural power of God into our financial lives—it's generosity.

The word *supernatural* implies that we have a practical part to play in God's supernatural work. **We must do what we can do, and then God will do what only He can do.** Many times, Jesus told a person to do something—a blind man to rub mud in his eyes, a lame man to get up, or a little boy to give up his lunch—and as they did these very natural things, miracles happened.

Generous, over-and-above giving is the natural thing we do to release supernatural blessings into our lives. There are two things we need to do regularly to unlock the supernatural in our finances. **First, be faithful where we are.** The principles and strategies outlined in the previous chapters work, so you should work them.

Second, give generously. Generosity isn't returning your tithe; that's simple obedience. **Generosity begins at eleven percent.** God doesn't just want to get resources *to* us. He wants to get resources *through* us. He has a plan to redeem the world. When we partner with God, we release supernatural blessing into our lives because God can trust us to be conduits of His blessing to others. **God multiplies whatever we put into His hands.**

- -

☐ **DAY 1**   **Ecclesiastes 9 and 2 Samuel 19**

☐ **DAY 2**   **Ecclesiastes 10 and 2 Samuel 20**

☐ **DAY 3**   **Ecclesiastes 11 and 2 Samuel 21**

☐ **DAY 4**   **Ecclesiastes 12 and 2 Samuel 22**

☐ **DAY 5**   **James 1–2 and 2 Samuel 23**

☐ **DAY 6**   **James 3–4 and 2 Samuel 24**

☐ **DAY 7**   **James 5, Titus 1–3**

⟲⟲⟲⟲⟲ REFLECT ⟲⟲⟲⟲⟲

1. How faithful are you with what God has entrusted to you? What natural things can you do to build and steward wealth God's way?

2. What do you need to put into Jesus' hands so that He can multiply it?

⟲⟲⟲⟲⟲ WRITE ⟲⟲⟲⟲⟲

Journal your thoughts from the discussion questions here.

CHAPTER NOTES

CONCLUSION

It is easy to look at our lives and get frustrated with where we are. One of the things I love about God is that He accepts us right where we are—problems and all. But the thing I love most about God is that He never leaves us the way He finds us. I want to encourage you in your moments of frustration, when it feels as if you took five steps forward and four-and-a-half steps back, to remember that nothing great comes easily or quickly. God has a plan for greatness designed for you as you put Him first and build your life on the solid foundation of His Word. As we wrap up this book, I want to give you some closing thoughts.

Wisdom Guides

As you come to a crossroad in your journey, financial or otherwise, you will be tempted to think you can take shortcuts to get ahead. Don't do it. It's always a trap. God has equipped you with the greatest resource for building and stewarding your entire life—wisdom that comes from His Word, the Bible. Everything else will pass away, but His Word remains. Don't just read it. Do it.

Diligence Builds

It doesn't matter where you're starting from, with hard work and perseverance you can get ahead. Work isn't a dirty word. Work is what converts God's wisdom into His blessings. Work hard and never stop learning and growing in skill and character. Growing in diligence will ensure that you're ready for everything God puts into your hands.

Honor Protects

Honor serves as a spiritual umbrella that covers your life. When you honor God, He protects you and everything you build. In every season of life, be determined to put God first and to honor the people He brings into your journey.

Faith Overcomes

Remember that building and stewarding wealth God's way won't eliminate every problem or setback. When you face financial obstacles, you are not alone. God is with you. He is good, and He will finish His work in you if you don't quit! With each victory, your faith will grow. Your obstacles will shrink when compared to the greatness of God and His work in your life.

A Wise Plan

Wisdom is better than money. Don't try to talk God into blessing you, just do what He already blesses. Use the principles of this book and the strategies you learn from other resources to help guide you on your journey. I encourage you to continue to study and grow in this area. Your plan will and should change over time. Remember that we plan, but God determines our steps for how we ultimately get there.

A Diligent Life

The life that God has for you won't come easily, but the blessing it brings is worth it. Keep your eyes on Jesus as you work hard and grow in skill and character. The rewards of a diligent life go beyond financial blessing and serve as a witness to those far from God. No one can keep a son or daughter of God down. Regardless of your circumstances, keep your heart right and your eyes up.

Honor First

The single greatest thing that's had the greatest return in my life has been to return the tithe to God. Something happens in your heart when you honor God in this way. Tithing leads to financial blessing, and it also brings God's blessings into every area of your life. When times are good, tithe. When times are bad, tithe. Honor God, regardless of your circumstances. Put Him first, and He will never let you down.

Generous Faith

You brought nothing into this world, and you won't take anything out of it, except the investment you made in building the kingdom of God. God only promised to build one thing, and it wasn't your 401K or your bank account, it was His Church. As you build His kingdom, He promises that your needs will be met, and He'll continue to supply seed for you to sow generously and to leave a legacy behind you.

The *WISER* life is a life that is built on God's Word.

My prayer for you is that you will discover God's plan for your life and walk in it fully and completely.

Sincerely,

Stephen

SECTION NOTES

A PRAYER FOR SALVATION

Jesus,

I need You. I am tired of living my way, and I want to choose Your way. Please help me. I invite You into my life to be my Lord and Savior. I believe what the Bible says about You is true. You are God. You came from Heaven to Earth. You lived a perfect life, and You died on the cross to forgive my sin, my failures, and my mistakes. I believe that three days after You were crucified, You rose from the dead and defeated death forever. I put my hope and trust in Your resurrection power. Come into my heart, and be my Lord and Savior. Change my life with the power of Your Holy Spirit. Thank You for meeting me where I am and for showing me a better way to live.

Amen.

OTHER RECOMMENDED RESOURCES

Better: My Life. God's Design.
by Stephen Martin

We want "better," and we want it now.

Americans spend billions of dollars every year in our efforts to get better. We want to be better today than we were yesterday and better tomorrow than we are today. We want next year to be better than last.

We're worried that we're not good enough and, no matter how hard we try, we can never measure up to everyone's expectations. We want to be better people, better friends, better husbands or wives, better parents. We want "better," and we want it now.

But what if the key to "better" isn't what we think it is? What if it doesn't start with us at all?

What if our concept of "better" isn't good enough?

With its essential life-application principles and in-depth personal and group study materials, *Better: My Life. God's Design.* by Stephen Martin is designed to help you learn the keys to "better" and discover that, with God's help, the better life you want is within your reach.

Order your copy of the book *Better: My Life. God's Design.* and the companion *Better Planner*™ at *betterplanner.com* today!

OTHER RECOMMENDED RESOURCES

The **Better Planner**™ is a thirteen-week personal planner designed to help you map out all the different aspects of success and personal growth on your way to better.

It can get complicated to make sure you're doing all the right things in all the right areas of life, but the **Better Planner**™ cuts through all the confusing apps and habit trackers, and puts the path to personal development right into the palm of your hands.

The **Better Planner**™ is radically different in its approach. By incorporating the seven biblical principles found in the book **Better: My Life. God's Design.** into one easy-to-use, thirteen-week planner, the **Better Planner**™ provides a framework for you to achieve success and follow God's plan for your life.

The foundation of the **Better Planner**™ is the practice of defining and reaching your personal vision. The other principles for growth all integrate with and flow out of this essential step.

As you develop and record the insights you receive from God and His design for your life, the **Better Planner**™ will lead you through a step-by-step process to become better.

To start your journey to better, order your copy of the **Better Planner**™ at *betterplanner.com* today!

ABOUT THE AUTHOR

Stephen Martin has been in ministry, serving the local church for more than twenty years. Born and raised in Tulsa, Oklahoma, Stephen began serving in ministry as a teenager, and then as an intern at his hometown church, Church On The Move. He went on to help with a local church plant and earn a bachelor's degree in interdisciplinary studies from Lindenwood University in Saint Louis, Missouri.

Stephen is passionate about serving and resourcing the local church—specifically church leaders. In 2009, he started One Church Resource, a global, online, sharing network for pastors, church leaders, and creatives.

In 2013, Stephen and his family moved to Texas and planted Vintage Church just outside of Fort Hood, the largest military base in the United States. Today, Vintage Church is a church of thousands and continues to make a significant impact in the Central Texas region. As the founder and Senior Pastor of this vibrant, growing congregation, Stephen firmly believes in its mission of *Reaching People and Building Lives*. He is dedicated to helping others take steps to grow into their God-given potential.

When he's not pastoring people or coaching leaders, Stephen loves spending time with his family, hunting deer, and reading. Stephen's wife, Kyla, is a Family Medicine Physician in the United States Army, and they have two beautiful daughters, Adilyn and Breelyn, and a son, Greyson.